Kawin, Bruce
F. 1945-
kner and film

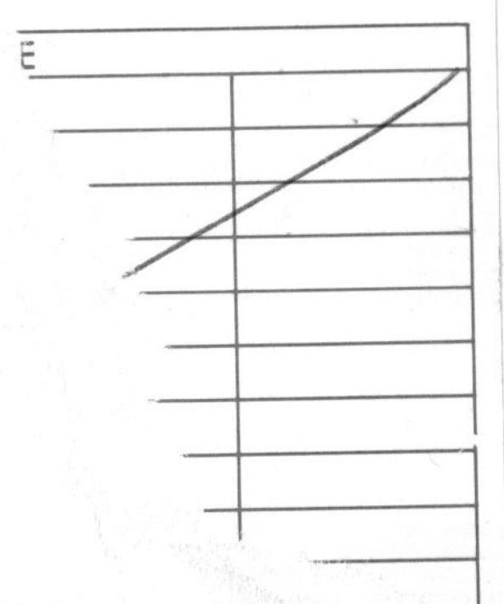

UNGAR FILM LIBRARY

STANLEY HOCHMAN, General Editor

The Classic American Novel and the Movies
Edited by Gerald Peary and Roger Shatzkin

Faulkner and Film
Bruce F. Kawin

Fellini the Artist
Edward Murray

Tennessee Williams and Film
Maurice Yacowar

Forthcoming:

The Modern American Novel and the Movies
Edited by Gerald Peary and Roger Shatzkin

On the Verge of Revolt: Women in American Films of the Fifties
Brandon French

Costume Design in the Movies
Elizabeth Leese

Theodore Dreiser, Sinclair Lewis, and Film
James Lundquist

Raymond Chandler and Film
Roger Shatzkin

Fitzgerald and Fil[illegible]
Philip Gordon

Other film books[illegible]

The Age of the A[illegible]
between the T[illegible]
Claude-Edmond[illegible]

The Cinematic Imagin[illegible]
Edward Murray

A Library of Film Criticis[illegible]
Edited by Stanley Hochma[illegible]

Nine American Film Critics
Edward Murray

FAULKNER AND FILM

BRUCE F. KAWIN

With halftone illustrations

FREDERICK UNGAR PUBLISHING CO.
New York

Printed in the United States of America
Designed by Lena Fong Hor

Library of Congress Cataloging in Publication Data

Kawin, Bruce F
Faulkner and film.

(Ungar film library)
Bibliography: p.
Filmography: p.
Includes index.
1. Faulkner, William, 1897–1962—Film adaptations.
2. Faulkner, William, 1897–1962—Criticism and interpretation. 3. Moving-pictures and literature. I. Title.
PS3511.A86Z859 813'.5'2 77-2519
ISBN 0-8044-2454-3
ISBN 0-8044-6347-6 pbk.

To

Howard Hawks

CONTENTS

Contents

ACKNOWLEDGMENTS

This book could not have been written without the help of a number of people. I particularly want to thank Howard Hawks for taking the time to talk with me and for sending me a copy of *Dreadful Hollow*, and Judy Zatkin for her helpful comments and enthusiastic encouragement throughout the project. James Powers, of the American Film Institute, helped me gain access to the studios. Herbert Nusbaum of MGM gave me the benefit of his legal advice; he and Jack Yaegar, of 20th Century-Fox, provided me with thousands of pages of screenplays and related documents from their story files. The staff members of the libraries at the University of California at Los Angeles, the University of Southern California, the Academy of Motion Picture Arts and Sciences, and the University of Colorado at Boulder were generous with their time and their holdings; I owe a great debt to Gladys Weibel, Robert Knutson, and Jim Wagner. Edmund Berkeley, Jr., Curator of Manuscripts at the University of Virginia's Alderman Library, provided me with the screenplays of *Revolt in the Earth* and *Stallion Road*; I want to thank him, Paul Levitt, and Charles Vandersee for making it possible for me to examine these "lost" manuscripts. The University of Colorado awarded me a CRCW Grant-in-Aid without which I could not have accomplished most of my research.

Many distributors sent me prints of their films at greatly reduced rates. I especially want to thank Paul Roebling for sending *Tomorrow*; Mike Swank of Swank Films for *The Reivers*; Budget Films for *The Southerner*; Macmillan/Audio-Brandon for *Sanctuary* and *Land of the Pha-*

raohs; Universal 16 for *The Tarnished Angels*; United Artists 16 for *The Amazing Dr. Clitterhouse*, *Air Force*, *To Have and Have Not*, *The Big Sleep*, and *Red River*; and Films, Inc., for delving into their archives in search of *Today We Live*, *The Road to Glory*, and *Banjo on My Knee*. Since I was denied access to Warner Brothers, I owe much to George Sidney for his lengthy descriptions of what he read there; I simply could not have written this book without his help, however indirect. Joseph Blotner was good enough to help me track down some hard information on Faulkner's early interest in the movies. Walter Slatoff, in a Cornell seminar, taught me how to read Faulkner in the first place. John Maas alerted me to the existence of *Tomorrow* and shared his thoughts on how a movie might have been made from *The Sound and the Fury*.

My colleagues at the University of Colorado were extremely supportive and helpful; my special thanks to Donald Baker, Bruce Bassoff, David Benson, James Folsom, Virgil Grillo, and Siegfried Mandel. Aladeen Smith worked with me for a full month on a transcript of the Hawks interview; she and Elsi Frederiksen typed the manuscript of this book during difficult times.

Finally, may I express my appreciation to Stan Hochman of Ungar for his encouragement and advice; Joan Gilbert, my agent, for her continuing enthusiasm and hard work on my behalf; Don Yannacito, for his help with the film rentals; David James, for his enlightened advice; Steven Axelrod, for pointing me in directions I never had considered; and Marian Keane, for teaching me more about montage than I taught her.

B.F.K.

Boulder, Colorado
December, 1976

CHRONOLOGY

1897 William Cuthbert Faulkner is born on September 25 in New Albany, Mississippi.

1902 Family moves from Ripley, Miss. to Oxford, Miss.

1914 Meets Phil Stone. Quits Oxford High School.

1918 Serves with RAF in Toronto, Canada.

1919 Signs his first published poem as William Faulkner. Enters University of Mississippi.

1920 Quits school for the last time.

1921 Clerks in a Greenwich Village bookstore.

1922 Begins work as postmaster in Oxford. Joyce's *Ulysses* and Eliot's *The Waste Land* published.

1924 First volume of poems, *The Marble Faun*, published. Meets Sherwood Anderson.

1925 Writes for a paper in New Orleans, then visits Europe.

1926 Lives in New Orleans. First novel, *Soldiers' Pay*, published.

1927 *Mosquitoes* published.

1928 Visits New York and revises *Flags in the Dust*. At work on *The Sound and the Fury*.

1929 *Sartoris* published. Marries Estelle Oldham shortly after her divorce. Works in power plant. *The Sound and the Fury* published.

1930 *As I Lay Dying* published.

1931 *Sanctuary* and *These 13* published. Daughter (Alabama) dies in infancy. Becomes famous; visits New York and meets Tallulah Bankhead.

1932 Begins work at MGM. Howard Hawks reads "Turn About" in *The Saturday Evening Post*. Scripts *Turn About* and begins *War Birds*. *Light in August* published.

1933 *A Green Bough* published. Daughter (Jill) born.

1934 Scripts *Sutter's Gold* at Universal. At work on *Absalom, Absalom! Doctor Martino and Other Stories* published.

1935 *Pylon* published. Brother (Dean) dies in plane accident. Begins work at 20th Century-Fox with *The Road to Glory*. Begins love affair with Meta Doherty Carpenter.

1936 *Absalom, Absalom!* published.

1938 *The Unvanquished* published.

1939 *The Wild Palms* published.

1940 *The Hamlet* published.

1942 *Go Down, Moses* published. Begins work at Warner Brothers. Scripts *The DeGaulle Story*, *Revolt in the Earth*, and part of *Air Force*.

1943 Scripts *Country Lawyer*, part of *Battle Cry*, and *Who?*

1944 Scripts *Fog over London* and parts of *To Have and Have Not*, *The Southerner*, and *The Big Sleep*.

1946 Malcolm Cowley's *Portable Faulkner* published.

1948 *Intruder in the Dust* published.

1949 *Intruder in the Dust* shot on location in Oxford. *Knight's Gambit* published.

1950 *Collected Stories* published. Wins 1949 Nobel Prize for Literature.

1951 Scripts *The Left Hand of God*. Wins National Book Award. *Requiem for a Nun* published.

1954 Scripts part of *Land of the Pharaohs* on location in Egypt. *A Fable* published.

1955 Wins National Book Award and Pulitzer Prize. *Big Woods* published.

1957 *The Town* published.

1959 *The Mansion* published.

1962 *The Reivers* published. Dies on July 6 of heart attack in Oxford, Miss.

1 FAULKNER, HAWKS, AND MONTAGE

In the late 1920s producer-director Howard Hawks read a novel that impressed him very much. Called *Soldiers' Pay*, it told the story of Donald Mahon, a lieutenant in the R.A.F. who was going blind from a wound he had received in the First World War, but who could remember neither the battle nor his sweetheart. The ambiguity of "glory" and the isolation of Mahon were presented in a clear and forceful way that appealed to Hawks, himself a former second lieutenant in the Army Air Corps. Hawks already had a reputation for recognizing talented writers, and was welcome at the New York salon of Ben Hecht and Charles MacArthur (authors of *The Front Page*). One evening he asked Hecht's crowd whether they had ever heard of the author of *Soldiers' Pay*, a Southerner named William Faulkner; they had not. "Well," said Hawks, "I think he's one of the most talented writers of this generation, and you ought to read him." The advice took, but those who went to their bookstores in search of *Soldiers' Pay* found instead a more recent work by that same author; it was around 1930, and the novel was *The Sound and the Fury*. They were impressed, began dropping his name, and "made him." On these grounds alone, the world "owes" Faulkner to Hawks, since without some kind of literary politicking, such an experimental (and personally reticent) writer would have had little chance of finding an audience.

In 1932 Hawks did Faulkner another service. He hadn't thought much of *The Sound and the Fury* or *As I Lay Dying*, but a new story by Faulkner in the *Saturday Evening Post* struck him as good material for a picture. He wrote to Faulkner and asked him to adapt that story, "Turn About," for the movies. Faulkner accepted, and thus markedly advanced his lagging career as a Hollywood screenwriter, in the course of which he worked on about fifty films and kept himself sufficiently solvent to write novels the way he wanted, regardless of commercial appeal. (This is not to suggest that he was comfortable and debt-free, but only that his Hollywood income kept him from starving.) From 1932 to 1954 he alternated between his hometown of Oxford, Mississippi, and Los Angeles, working at one time or another with Jean Renoir, Irving Thalberg, Darryl F. Zanuck, Nunnally Johnson, and Jules Furthman; he even reworked a project first tackled in 1930 by the brilliant Russian director, Sergei Eisenstein. He collaborated, notably, on *The Big Sleep*, *To Have and Have Not*, *The Southerner*, *The Road to Glory*, and *Air Force*, and in addition wrote thousands of pages of scripts that were never produced, several of which extend and vary the themes of his major fiction, but which have never found a wide audience, either scholarly or popular.[1]

Faulkner's screenplay for *War Birds*, for instance, tells part of the story of the Sartoris family, and properly belongs in his cycle of works on the inhabitants of the mythical Yoknapatawpha County. His contributions to *The Big Sleep* (many of which did not reach the screen) build on the themes of *The Sound and the Fury*, converting Raymond Chandler's nymphomaniac villainess (Carmen Sternwood) into a version of Quentin II, the doomed daughter of a proud and decaying Southern family. *The Road to Glory*, which he and Hawks adapted from a French film about war in the trenches, not only boasts a suicidal romantic whose greatest love is for his lost sister (an echo of *The Sound and the Fury's* Quentin Compson, the uncle of Quentin II), but also dramatizes the cyclical view of time and history that is implicit, but much harder to pin down, in many of his novels. His religious preoccupations, which tend to be buried in the symbolic structures and titles of such novels as *Absalom, Absalom!* and *Sanctuary*, are played out in the open in much of his Hollywood work—to the extent that his most forthright religious tract, the novel *A Fable*, actually began as a screenplay.

In the collaborative and visual art of film it is hard to pin down what an individual writer might have been responsible for, even when he is given solo credit as adaptor or screenwriter. In that famous scene in *To Have or Have Not*, where Lauren Bacall leans in the doorway and asks Bogart for a light, or when she tells him that if he wants her all he has to do is whistle ("You know how to whistle, don't you, Steve? You just put your lips together and blow"), the sexy power of these scenes was called for by Hawks, and depends largely on the fact that Bacall and Bogart were really falling in love with each other at the time; "You just couldn't get their attention," as Hawks explained it to me. The dialogue was written by Jules Furthman (who had had a lot of practice at it, in his scripts for Marlene Dietrich and Josef von Sternberg), by Hawks, and by an uncredited, six-foot-two chorus girl whom Hawks called "Stuttering Sam." And the characters were, marginally, the creation of Ernest Hemingway, who wrote the original novel and collaborated with Hawks on the preliminary outline (treatment) of the screenplay. What Faulkner did, in this case, was to figure out the staging of the scenes—the device of the facing doorways, which made the casualness of these encounters possible. (He also provided, in *As I Lay Dying*, the model for the narrative structure of Hemingway's novel—a structure that is nowhere evident in the film.)

So the question of who did what, and why, becomes fairly complex, and in making such determinations I have depended not so much on critics and biographers (who tend to dismiss the seriousness of this aspect of Faulkner's career in the first place) as on firsthand accounts by the people who worked on these films, on Faulkner's penciled notes in the margins of those screenplays and first drafts that survive in the studio vaults, and on the resemblance of an occasional preoccupation or line of dialogue to some memorable scene in a novel.

But this is not simply a study of Faulkner's career as a screenwriter. Rather it is an attempt to explore the interactions between literature and film, using Faulkner as test case—not only because he worked in both media (since the same could be observed of F. Scott Fitzgerald, Nathanael West, Raymond Chandler, James Agee, Alain Robbe-Grillet, Norman Mailer, Susan Sontag, and others), but also because he is the most cinematic of novelists. Such techniques as montage, freeze-frame, slow motion, and visual metaphor abound in his fiction. Moreover, he is a novelist read by filmmakers from Howard Hawks to Jean-Luc Godard (whose sometime favorite novel is *The Wild Palms*)—one who is demonstrably an influence on the resurgence of personal, experimental film in France in the late 1950s (the New Wave), and who therefore has an important place in *film* history. It is even arguable that Faulkner picked up these techniques from film itself, or from writers who were, as Gertrude Stein put it, "doing what the cinema was doing."[2]

The most notable of these writers are James Joyce, T. S. Eliot, and John Dos Passos, and Faulkner is known to have taken all three seriously. One knows of his interest in Dos Passos, for instance, from a story Hawks tells of a dove-hunting expedition, during which he and Faulkner talked about contemporary literature. Their companion, Clark Gable, was not particularly well read, and he asked Faulkner whom he considered the best living writers. The response was, "Ernest Hemingway, Willa Cather, Thomas Mann, John Dos Passos, and William Faulkner." "Do you write, Mr. Faulkner?" asked Gable, and Faulkner replied, "Yes, Mr. Gable; what do you do?"

Faulkner's debts to Joyce and Eliot are more immediately obvious in his work. He often alludes to "The Love Song of J. Alfred Prufrock" or "The Waste Land" in novels as diverse as *Pylon, As I Lay Dying*, and *Mosquitoes*. And Joyce's semi-autobiographical hero, Stephen Dedalus, is the basic model for Faulkner's Quentin Compson. More to the point, however, is the fact that Joyce's

Ulysses, Eliot's "The Waste Land," Dos Passos's *U.S.A.*, and by far the majority of Faulkner's experimental fiction all depend to varying extents on a single, recurring technique—montage. It would not be precise to insist on montage as an exclusively cinematic device; rather, it is a structural principle used by writers and filmmakers throughout the century, and for approximately the same purposes. Since the aesthetics of montage are basic to the whole question of how literature and film interact (both in history and in theory), and since they are at the heart of Faulkner's work, it is necessary at this point to show how the writers and filmmakers of the 1920s used and thought about montage.

"Montage" began as a general term for film editing, the art of "mounting" one shot next to another. In the hands of the Russian film theorists, it took on the more specialized meaning of *dynamic juxtaposition*. One image, or shot, or signifier, is butted up against another, with no transitional apparatus, and it is left to the audience to divine the connection between the two elements. In a "montage sequence," these signifiers may follow one another in great number and with extreme rapidity. It is not the speed of cutting that determines what is or is not montage, however, but the ways the connections between shots are established. In D. W. Griffith's 1916 film *Intolerance*, for example, four stories from four different epochs are told at once. The audience is yanked from a Babylonian battle scene to a Reformation massacre to a contemporary cell on Death Row to the Crucifixion, with very little explanation of how the stories relate. This process of juxtaposition has a powerful kinetic effect, but it also has meaning, in that it forces the audience to explore the *general* nature of intolerance—which is mainly, for

Griffith, the denial of another's right to love or play or worship in new ways. (Most of these issues are presented as class conflicts, however, in which the rich and powerful oppress the gentle poor; this accounts for the special interest taken in this film by the Russians.)

Like any system, a film is more than the sum of its parts. In this case, the film's meaning is created by the montage—that is to say, by the interrelation of its parts (the four stories). Intolerance, as an abstraction, cannot be photographed—cannot be a "part" of the film, but can be suggested by what *can* be photographed. A similar problem arises with metaphor. It is difficult, in film, to say "this is *like* that," unless the two things happen to look the same or can be handled in relatable ways. By cross-cutting between a workers' demonstration as it courses through the streets and a parallel surge of ice-floes down a river, V. I. Pudovkin, for instance (at the climax of his 1926 film, *Mother*), establishes a connection between the rise of the proletariat and the way the spring thaw destroys the lock of winter. Film metaphor, then, tends to work in a way different from verbal metaphor. The elements of film metaphor, and the dynamics of their interrelation, must be *visually* presented.

Griffith's montage on the nature of intolerence lasts almost three hours. His counterpart, the French director Abel Gance, tended to make his points rather more quickly. In his 1926 masterpiece, *Napoléon*, it is common to find hundreds of shots going by in a few minutes, some of them only a tenth of a second in length. At one point Gance intercuts shots of Napoleon's controlling a small boat in a storm with shots of Robespierre's purging a rival party in the French revolutionary assembly. The camera swings and pitches through the assembly, making it clear that this too is a kind of storm; but the continual juxtaposition of the two "storms," and of the faces of Napoleon and Robespierre, suggests an abstract point about two kinds of political control, and illuminates Napoleon's role in French history. (In one version of *Napoléon*, these sequences were presented simultaneously, on a Cinerama screen; the surviving version uses the more conventional device of rapid intercutting.) Faulkner used a simpler version of *Intolerance*'s montage in his novel *The Wild Palms* (where two stories are told in alternating chapters), and a variation on Gance's kind of montage in the opening sections of *The Sound and the Fury*.

The Russian directors studied the works of Griffith and Gance very carefully, and produced a substantial body of film theory. The most widely read of these men was Sergei Eisenstein, the director of *Battleship Potemkin* and *October (Ten Days that Shook the World)*. Eisenstein, who is mentioned by name in *The Wild Palms*, and who was greatly admired by Dos Passos, was also Joyce's choice to be director of *Ulysses* (a project that never came off). He is the major theorist of montage, and his work on the subject deserves special attention here.

Eisenstein emphasized that the elements of a montage ought not to build on each other but to *collide*, and that this process was essentially dialectical. In *October*, for instance, a shot of a dead horse's fall from a rising drawbridge is juxtaposed with a shot of a Bolshevist banner's being thrown into the river by a group of enraged bourgeois. The point is not that horse and banner are the same kind of revolutionary symbol—they are not—but that the viewer, forced to confront both falling actions at once, arrives at a more general, abstract conception of the way the Kerensky government betrayed the original impulse of the Russian Revolution; the bourgeois are perceived as a new kind of oppressor. The horse shot (A) and the banner shot (B) are juxtaposed on screen so that they collide in the audience's mind, where a concept (C) arises. It is in this sense that the process is dialectical: thesis (A) interacts with antithesis (B) to produce a synthesis (C), which in its turn becomes a new thesis (A′), etc. The work of achieving this synthesis is left to the viewer, not because the artist is lazy but because he is ambitious. In many cases the A and B are concrete, but the C is abstract, or undiscovered, or—in Eisenstein's phrase—"graphically undepictable." In most cases the collision itself is a kind of synthesis; this art of *un*resolution, when it proceeds from a clear mind, is extremely stimulating.

One can observe this process in an early poem by Ezra Pound, "In a Station of the Metro." The first line presents an image of "faces in the crowd," and the second line describes flower petals on a "wet, black bough." End of poem. Between the two lines there is only a semicolon, and it is the crucial element. The two images are maintained in balance; they do not equal each other or explain each other, as a colon might have implied. They simply co-exist. It is not so much a simile or a metaphor as a double—or doubled—perception. A and B yield C, but C is not *in* the poem.

Interestingly enough, both Pound and Eisenstein explained their techniques the same way, by referring to the structure of the ideogram. Pound admired the way the Chinese hieroglyph for "red" is composed of the abbreviated hieroglyphs of four red things; no red paint is used, but the intention to signify redness is clear from the juxtaposition. (This is precisely the way Griffith's four stories deal with "intolerance.") Eisenstein's major paper on montage begins with a demonstration of how the Japanese signify "to weep" by putting together the signifiers for water and for the eye.[3] These two men may not have read each other, but a great many other artists were influenced by their example.

Both Joyce and Eliot were discovered, and at times kept financially solvent, by Pound, who was also quite free with his advice; he did a major job of editing on "The Waste Land," and was consulted by Joyce throughout the composition of *Ulysses*. His own great poem, *The Cantos*, is (like William Carlos Williams's *Paterson*) a montage epic. Dos Passos, who was familiar with all these writers, considered Eisenstein's *Potemkin* an enormous influence on his own work and on that of his colleagues. And at the time that all this was happening, Faulkner was in Paris, sitting at the feet of the great.

Before his European tour in 1925–26, Faulkner had been a fairly derivative novelist. *Soldiers' Pay* and *Mosquitoes* are conventionally structured, for all the talent they reveal; his poetry is frankly boring and effete. Biographers and critics are always searching for the mysterious impetus or influence that made it possible for him, almost immediately upon his return to the States, to become such a major writer. Within a year of that return he had invented the principal characters of his Yoknapatawpha cycle (in *Flags in the Dust*, later published as *Sartoris*), and within the next three years he had written *The Sound and the Fury* and *As I Lay Dying*. It seems possible to argue that what he discovered was montage—that it fit his sensibility, and made possible the expression of his most complex and troubling convictions. For what is most essential in Faulkner's experimental fiction is the way characters and events repeat and collide with no regard for the conventions of chronology. All time is equal, all mental space accessible, right up to the edge of a cosmic, ineffable silence.

What is basic to Modernism, to the work of all these writers, and to montage, is the sense that the old world of shared values, live traditions, constructive politics, and smooth forms is kaput. The world these artists confronted lay in pieces, and only by yoking these fragments into a new system could they invent for themselves some kind of viable culture. "The Waste Land," for instance, juxtaposes short scenes, elliptical meditations, allusions to old poems and cultures, and wildly varying tones—refusing to show how they interrelate, but generating accurately the feel of the Modernist world, which exists in some foregone relation to the realm of continuity and value. By the same token, *Ulysses* constructs its modern adventurer, Leopold Bloom, out of a whole complex of heroes and father-figures, notably Shakespeare, Socrates, King Hamlet, the middle-aged Joyce himself, and of course Odysseus. The city Bloom walks through is a montage of Avon, Athens, Elsinore, the Mediterranean, and the knowable universe, as well as "dear, dirty Dublin." For Joyce, as for Eliot, the most viable tone is parody. Bloom (A) collides absurdly with Odysseus (B), but the option of simply presenting a modern mythic hero (C as A′) is not open. Similarly, the closest Faulkner will allow himself to come to a portrait of a saintly innocent is the idiot Compson, Benjy; parody, however, is not his intention, nor one of his basic tones. As we shall see, *The Sound and the Fury* refuses to cohere even more rigorously than "The Waste Land" or *Ulysses*; for Faulkner, montage—the dynamic suspension of conflicting elements—can be accepted on its own terms, not as a way-station on the road to synthesis, but as a revelatory and viable state of mind. As he presents it, consciousness may be a "stream," but it is a stream of fragments. Past collides with present, reality with fantasy, interior monologue with spoken dialogue, one mind with another, one story with another. The unscrambled story, divorced from the montage technique that focuses all this energy, rarely appears worth bothering about.

This raises the question of the movies that have been made from Faulkner's novels, and of Faulkner's attitude toward movies and movie-makers. Howard Hawks has always shunned both montage and flashbacks, and only rarely has he attempted to tell more than one story at once—but almost the opposite is true of Faulkner. How did they work together? Did Faulkner come to Hollywood with Eisenstein and Joyce on his mind, or was he—as Hawks believes—ignorant of film at the time? It is possible that he saw montage as a strictly literary technique, and agreed with Hawks that the function of filmmaking was simply to tell good stories, but it is also possible that he understood all these connections but left Hollywood to the producers' box-office aesthetics and experimental filmmaking to the Europeans. Whatever the reason, the majority of his screenplays tell their stories straightforwardly, using montage—if at all—only as a transitional device. And the stories he told were good ones. They were also often considerably more coherent *and* interesting than the films that have been made from his major novels.

The fault with these adaptations may be that they attempt to present "what Faulkner meant," and to tell the novels' basic stories, without sticking to—or finding a suitable equivalent for—the techniques that made those stories work in the first place. In the case of *The Sound and the Fury*, more immediate faults come to mind: notably the producer's and writers' failure to understand or *care* about the story, let alone to approach it with any kind of talent or integrity. But even so poor a film as this one can reveal much about our subject; it is such a *total* failure that it points out, by contrast, the cinematic nature of the original novel, and suggests better ways the project might have been tackled.

One is struck then, at first glance, by a paradox: Faulkner's novels are cinematic, and his screenplays are novelistic. To explore this crossover, let us start with the problem of adaptation: how do Faulkner's novels look on the screen? Do their cinematic qualities transfer to film itself—has that attempt, in fact, even been made? And when Faulkner wrote his own treatment for *Absalom, Absalom!*, one of his most difficult novels, why did he *not* do a better job than producer Jerry Wald and screenwriters Irving Ravetch and Harriet Frank, Jr. did on *The Sound and the Fury*? Where the adaptations are poor, is the fault in the novels or in Hollywood's approach to them? And how did Faulkner deal with, say, the novels of Hemingway and Chandler when he was assigned the task of adapting *them*?

We have already observed some of the ways in which film and modern literature are able to resemble each other structurally, and some of the ways they fundamentally diverge. It should be of interest, in the next two chapters, to see how works in both media deal with approximately the same stories and problems. At that point it should be possible to evaluate Faulkner's career as a screenwriter, and to discover what film, as an art, might have meant to him, and what he has meant to film.

2

THE SOUND AND THE FURY

Although its title might be taken to suggest otherwise, the principal theme of *The Sound and the Fury* is the nature of order. The perceptions and emotions of its characters tend to be chaotic, and the structure of the narrative is scrambled; what most of the characters want, however, is for the world to conform to their *ideas* of it, and each section of the novel is written in a progressively clearer, more objective manner than the one before. Yet even as the story becomes easier to understand, its implications become more troubling, so that at its eloquent, "ordered" finish one is left with the impression that the novel's first, confusing pages are in their own way the most true and simple. (Quentin Compson, for instance, enters "real" time by breaking his watch.)

In its broadest outlines, the novel's story is as follows. Jason Compson, a dipsomaniac, and Caroline Bascomb Compson, a whining and manipulative remnant of Southern belle gentility, have four children. The eldest son, Quentin, is a moody intellectual; the daughter, Caddy, is hot-blooded and self-destructive, but also the bravest and most compassionate of the Compsons; the next son, Jason, is a crybaby in childhood and a domineering materialist in adulthood; the youngest, Maury—named after his mother's brother, an alcoholic-in-residence—is extremely sensitive but a congenital idiot. When Maury's retardedness is discovered, the mother changes his name to Benjy. This family of frantic and selfish losers is looked after by Dilsey, a Negro servant whose more "enduring" virtues are wisdom, compassion, and ethical autonomy.

All three brothers are fixated on Caddy. Each of them views the world in rigid terms, and expresses this by trying to control Caddy—who is herself, however, the essence of risk and change; the battleground is her maidenhead. Quentin appears incestuously attracted to Caddy, and does everything he can to prevent her from sleeping with a local rake, Dalton Ames—even to the point of proposing a suicide pact. The issue is not really incest, but his sense that her loss of virginity would entail the fall of all the values in which he wants to believe: the honor of the family, the permanence of chastity, and the endurance of history—all of which add up, as Faulkner has explained, to a love of death. But Caddy will not be contained, and gets pregnant by Ames. This is the key event in the lives of all the characters, and is foreshadowed by a scene that Faulkner considered crucial. In that scene Caddy, aged seven, had been playing with her brothers in the branch of a creek, and had deliberately muddied her underpants. When she took off her dress to dry it, Quentin slapped her;

Caddy then broke another rule by climbing a tree to look in on her grandmother's wake. Faulkner has said that this book is essentially the story of a little girl who dirtied her drawers, and the principal themes of this scene—sex, death, control, and rebellion—are clearly central to the novel.

Benjy loves three things: Caddy, the shape of fire, and the family pasture. Benjy loses title to this pasture just as Quentin loses his hold on the more abstract field of the family's honor. In 1909 the pasture is sold to a golf club to provide enough money to send Quentin to Harvard, and Caddy is seduced by Dalton Ames; in 1910 she marries an obnoxious banker, Sydney Head. At the end of his freshman year, on June 2, 1910, Quentin drowns himself in the Charles River, primarily because he cannot bear the fact of change. Caddy gives birth to a daughter, names her Quentin in her brother's memory, and—divorced by the banker—leaves her infant to be raised by the Compsons. It is at this point that her brother Jason suffers *his* major loss, which is of the promise of a position in Sydney Head's bank; furious with Caddy, he focuses his resentment on Quentin II. After his father's death, Jason becomes the head of the family; Caddy sends him money for Quentin II's support, and he embezzles most of it.

The main action of the novel takes place during Easter in 1928, when Quentin II goes the route of her mother. The novel's first section takes place inside Benjy's head on Saturday, April 7, 1928. As Benjy has no way of distinguishing past from present, and does not know the names for most of the things he sees, his section is fairly hard to follow. The look and smell and sound of things, not their intellectual aspects, are presented directly as they occur to him. Whenever he is reminded of the loss of his sister—by

a golfer's yelling "Caddie!" for instance—he begins to bellow. Among other things, he notices Quentin II with her prospective seducer; that night, as he is going to sleep, he sees her climbing down a tree, out of the room in which she has been locked by her mother.

The second section is narrated by Quentin on the day of his suicide in 1910. Unlike Benjy, he *can* keep time straight, but it is just this oversensitivity to time and history that destroys him. Like Benjy, he continually flashes back to earlier events, and even to fantasies, but his section is easier to understand because he can articulate and explain himself. On the other hand, he is so caught up in the pressure of his abstractions that his stream of consciousness is not just chaotic and allusive, but frankly psychotic—a labyrinth in an earthquake.

The third section is narrated by Jason, who is—to say the least—neither as sensitive as Benjy nor as intelligent as Quentin; its action takes place on Good Friday, April 6, 1928. Here it is established that Jason has been stealing the child-support money, that Quentin II is flirting with a man with a red tie (in town with a carnival), that Jason had had Benjy castrated and intends to send him to an asylum, and that the household is being held together only by Jason's dominance and Dilsey's endurance. Jason is easy to understand, but a crass and vindictive, vicious, rigid figure.

The fourth and final section is narrated in the third person (maximum clarity) and takes place on Sunday, April 8, 1928 (maximum temporal stability). While Dilsey takes Benjy to an Easter service, Jason discovers that Quentin II has run away with the carnival man—and, more important, with the money he has been saving for seventeen years, some of it rightfully hers, and some of it his own. He chases her, unsuccessfully. On the way back he sees Luster, Dilsey's grandson, driving Benjy through the town square. In the center of the square is a Confederate monument, which Benjy is accustomed to pass on the right. Luster has turned to the left, upsetting the order, and Benjy has started to bellow. Jason turns the horse around; with everything once again in its proper place, Benjy is happy. On that note the novel ends, but the impression is hardly one of stability or resolution.

The novel establishes a dialectic between rigidity and death on the one hand, and flexibility, compassion, life, and strength on the other. Most of the latter virtues fall to Dilsey, and to Caddy's first plans for herself; the obsessed brothers hold up the other end. The irony is that their demand for order generates most of the chaos, so that the novel becomes much calmer when it deals with Dilsey. Nevertheless, at its most peaceful moment—Benjy's vision of order as he passes the monument on the correct path—the novel is at the height of its crazy irony, since the vision is not of order but of habit and control and denial. It is a moment of untruth, whereas the opening pages present the world without "interpretation," but also without distortion. It is the tale told by the idiot that, for all its sound and fury, signifies most. This dialectic—finally between life and death—focuses the novel, suspends its issues, excites and troubles the reader, and dooms the characters: like Caddy, who is caught and pulled in so many directions that she can only choose life and guilt, and find damnation.

The collision of these elements is accomplished through three kinds of montage. First, the four sections—which proceed from different minds, center on different days, and vary drastically in tone and technique—are butted against each other without explanation. Second, the contradictory implications of such scenes as the final one are dynamically suspended through the rhetorical and structural device of the extended oxymoron (as Walter Slatoff has demonstrated in his fine study, *Quest for Failure*[1]). Third, past and present and even fantasy are rapidly and repeatedly intercut, within the streams of consciousness of Benjy and Quentin. The latter experience great "freedom" in time, the one because he cannot discriminate between what is happening and what is remembered, the other because he cannot simply live in the developing present and has even smashed his watch as a gesture of metaphysical rebellion.

Joyce used this third type of montage throughout *Ulysses*, and an example from that novel might help to clarify what Faulkner is doing here. At one point the hero of *Ulysses*, Leopold Bloom, is drinking a glass of Burgundy in a bar, half-listening to the buzzing of two flies that are stuck on a window and evidently copulating. The wine on his palate brings to his mind the effect of the sun on the grape, and suddenly he is off on a memory of the sunny heath where he first made love to Molly, his future wife. He comes out of it this way:

> All yielding she tossed my hair. Kissed, she kissed me.
> Me. And me now.
> Stuck, the flies buzzed.
> His downcast eyes followed the silent veining of the oaken slab. Beauty: it curves, curves are beauty.[2]

Two montages are at work here: present with past, and first person with third, never as overlap but in succession.

At the climax of the second section of *The Sound and the Fury*, Quentin picks a fight with a student at a picnic, while remembering his fight with Caddy's seducer, Dalton Ames. Both fights are presented in a montage that includes his memory of a third, crucial scene—one that Faulkner managed to include, with variations, in several of his screenplays. In that scene, which Quentin has presumably been remembering in both of his fights, Caddy attempts to prove to her brother the intensity of her passion for Ames, by making him feel the pulse in her neck:

> put your hand against my throat
> she took my hand and held it flat against her throat
> now say his name
> Dalton Ames
> I felt the first surge of blood there it surged in strong accelerating beats
> say it again
> her face looked off into the trees where the sun slanted and where the bird
> say it again
> Dalton Ames
> her blood surged steadily beating and beating against my hand
> It kept on running for a long time, but my face felt cold and sort of dead, and my eye, and the cut place on my finger was smarting again. I could hear Shreve working the pump, then he came back with the basin. . . .[3]

Shreve is Quentin's roommate at Harvard. Like Bloom, Quentin has come back from a memory that is as real as the present, during which what he thought and said and heard have been separated from each other only by line-breaks, which are in this case the equivalent of straight cuts. No dissolves or fades or whirly opticals (outmoded

Hollywood conventions for separating event from dream, or one time from another) are necessary. These flashes of events butt together on the page as they do in Quentin's mind, and the effect is entirely cinematic—which is to say that it could be filmed, and be clear, without modification. When it *was* filmed, however, this montage technique was abandoned, and with it the meaning and energy of the novel.

In 1955 Jerry Wald, who had bought the screen rights to *The Hamlet* and *The Sound and the Fury* (along with several other "high-class" literary properties), offered Faulkner the chance to adapt these novels himself, but Faulkner refused on the grounds that he didn't need the money. As far as he was concerned, he had already said what he wanted to say, in the novels. Even if Faulkner had taken the job, however, it is unlikely that Wald would have given him a free hand, let alone encouraged him to stick to the techniques and structures of the originals.

It is one thing to feel, like Hawks, that a film ought to tell a story clearly and in chronological order, and another to have the talent to do that job well. In the case of Jerry Wald, such conservatism could become obnoxious (as well as pretentious and low-brow) when coupled with what was at times an extraordinary lack of artistic *and* commercial intelligence.[4] The screenwriters to whom he assigned these projects—the husband-and-wife team of Irving Ravetch and Harriet Frank, Jr.—apparently had some kind of respect for Faulkner's work, and later produced on their own a decent adaptation of *The Reivers*. But they shared with Wald his initial assumption that the only part of *The Sound and the Fury* that *could* be brought or was worth bringing to the screen was its plot. And they did a poor job in even that department.

The principal theme of the film, *The Sound and the Fury* (1959), is maturity, in a rather limited sense of the word. It is now the story of Quentin II's rebellion against her step-uncle, Jason. He wants her to be respectable, to hold her head up in Jefferson in spite of her shady parentage; she wants him to leave her alone. (Or: she wants to be Betty, and he wants her to be Veronica.) By the end of the film, she has decided not to run away with the carnival man, Charlie Busch, but to seduce Jason—who was right all along—into marrying her. Where the credo of Faulkner's Jason is "Once a bitch, always a bitch," the advice of this Jason (played by Yul Brynner) to his willful charge (played by Joanne Woodward) is "Knowledge is power; get out and be good." Where the organizing interest of the novel is in its complex treatment of time, Wald and the Ravetches felt it was essential to tell the whole story "in the present," which is defined as a few weeks in the mid-1950s. To keep Quentin and Caddy in the story, and avoid the confusion of multiple Quentins, the former is recast as Uncle Howard (alcoholic-in-residence) and the latter returns from her travels to live with the family. To make it possible for Quentin II and Jason to contemplate a sexual relationship—and to justify the casting of Yul Brynner—Jason's mother is presented as Mr. Compson's second wife, a Cajun. The sound and fury are recast as sexual tension and domestic anger; the music is "torrid," but the visual style is placid. Benjy, played in silence by Jack Warden, is a vaguely menacing figure into whom we get no insight. Caddy (Margaret Leighton) pathetically echoes, in her lines and demeanor, Blanche DuBois, the tragic heroine of Tennessee Williams's *A Streetcar Named Desire*, as if Blanche were the only image of a promiscuous Southern ex-lady the adaptors could conjure up. For all the abuse heaped on Brynner by reviewers and critics, it is Leighton who sinks the film—followed in close rank by the saccharine Woodward. And although the script is juvenile and wooden, Martin Ritt's direction is downright inept. There is no evidence here that Ritt might go on to make *Hud* or *The Great White Hope*, nor even that he might already have made the relatively clear and forceful *Edge of the City* and *The Long, Hot Summer*. The flaws that most concern us here, however, are in the basic conception of the screenplay, for which Wald and the Ravetches are mutually culpable.

Their operating method was to retain as many of the novel's scenes and characters as possible, rearranging and recasting them in the narrative present. The problem is that they kept the surfaces and lost the meanings—and even this would not be so much of a problem if the new meanings they created had been dramatically interesting. It is not proper to attack an adaptation for being *different* from its source; the changes must be evaluated in their own terms. *To Have and Have Not*, for instance, relates as little to Hemingway's novel as *The Long, Hot Summer* does to Faulkner's *The Hamlet*, yet each achieves its own legitimacy.

Caddy's "doom," for example, has in the novel a wide range of cultural and psychological implications. Sexual restlessness is among the forces bearing her and her brother, Quentin, to a destruction so large that Faulkner is able—in an Appendix he wrote to the novel in 1945—to relate it to the rise of Nazism in Europe without appearing to be stretching a point. A similar tragic sense is at work in Williams's *Streetcar*, which may even be in Faulkner's debt. But Margaret Leighton's Caddy suffers simply from unrespectability. And although it is arguable that if Quentin had not killed himself he might have grown into an alcoholic lawyer like Uncle Howard, it is ludicrous to have him and Caddy play out, in their late forties, a scene that can make sense only in Quentin's youth—the "Dalton Ames" episode quoted above. Yet there it is: Caddy and Howard by the branch, Howard demanding, "How many were there? Did you love them? Did you? Did you love them?" and Caddy crying, "Shut up. You shut up! You hear me? Are you going to shut up?" This exchange is precipitated by Caddy's memory of getting her drawers wet and *Dilsey's* yelling at her, to which Howard responds by describing his fight with Dalton Ames. Part of the trouble is that this is all *talk*, an allusion to two good scenes in another work, motivated not by the drama of the moment but by the adaptors' refusal to employ flashbacks. As if to make up for this, the rest of the "Dalton Ames" scene is acted out on camera—but it takes place between Quentin II and Jason!

After leaving Howard, Caddy buys some presents for Jason and a package of bath oil for herself, then seduces Jason's boss, Earl. "It's so hot in here," she complains to him, as woozy music comes on the soundtrack; "A sweet little boy offered to take me home," she says, as the music turns eerie—all of this straight from Elia Kazan's *Streetcar* (1951). Later, Earl drops her at home and tells Jason, "Even if the name is Compson, after closing time they're all the same." Jason defends the family honor by beating up Earl, then hears Quentin II making out with Charlie the carnival pitchman (played with absurdly introspective vigor by Stuart Whitman). Jason chases Charlie away, then grabs Quentin II's neck and demands, "What's his name?" "Charlie Busch!" "Say it again!" he orders. "Charlie Busch!" "Again!" "Charlie Busch!" "I feel the pulse jumping in your throat—every time you say it," he says, sadistically. "What are you going to do about it?" she cries. "I'll slow it down," he says, and kisses her, to prove that "*Anybody* could make you feel like a woman." She, of course, returns the kiss.

The point of Faulkner's scene is Caddy's attempt to force her brother to realize that she is passionate, by having him feel the pulse in her neck as he, on *her command*, says the lover's name. Here the power structure has been reversed, and the scene's point becomes the conflict between male worldliness and female vulnerability. This method of adaptation reaches its maximum inappropriateness when Jason sends Benjy off to an asylum where he can be happy, after Benjy has attempted to strangle Quentin II. "Benjamin, the last born—" he emotes, "sold into Egypt." This is of course Quentin's line in the novel, an intellectual's meditation on an innocent. It might be worth pointing out, too, that Faulkner's Jason has Benjy castrated for approaching a bunch of schoolgirls in a manner that is misinterpreted as threatening, and is just dying to send Benjy off to an asylum so that he can be rid of him; Jason is simply waiting for the rest of the family to leave or die off so that he can live as he pleases. The adaptors had to have a hero, so they took Jason; they had to have a heroine, so they let Quentin II grow into the part. When the film's Jason discovers that Quentin II has stolen "his" money, he lets her keep it—he was just going to spend it on her anyway. And so it goes.

What the film adds up to, then, is a conventional demonstration of the value of convention; its battle is the battle for respectability, which Quentin II, under the admittedly nasty guidance of Jason, wins—and which her mother loses. (So much for Faulkner's aesthetic of repetition!)

Jason's controlling tactics—cutting down the tree outside Quentin II's window, for instance—are informed by his dedication to positive nurturance. The Compsons are not his kin, but as he says, they'd better "hang on to me—I'm all you've got!" Caddy's dragging down the family name, it seems, is reversible; all that is needed is a little domination, a little order. Although Wald defended their screenplay for its accessible presentation of "the *spirit* and *essence* of the original," it is clear that the adaptors have presented exactly the opposite of that spirit and essence.

"Accessibility" is the key here. In their studio memo, "On Putting Faulkner on the Screen,"[5] the Ravetches argue that "It is clearly impossible to bring Faulkner to the screen by just writing camera angles into the body of his scenes and then going out to shoot them." In fact, if the novel is as cinematic as I have argued, this should not be the case. The point is that the Ravetches have a less formalist sense of what "cinematic" means; to them it is simply a term for that which will be visually and intellectually accessible to "a vast and miscellaneous audience." Nor is this an unfortunate definition—the problem is that they underestimate that audience, and are using their image of the dumb public to justify not only their oversimplifications but also their inventions. They present ideas only in words, having no feel for visual metaphor or for intellectually significant conflict. Confronted with a complexity, they seize on a cliché—hence the blanching of Caddy, and the conversion of Quentin II into a 1950s adolescent with self-respectful "ideas about sex."

As a test case for what *might* have been done, let us examine the scenes the adaptors considered most inaccessible: those that take place in the mind of Benjy. He shifts among times and places too abruptly for them, and has no words with which to express his feelings. Clearly their method of putting the whole story into what they call "the present," and of telling it in the third person, mandates against any imitation of Faulkner's experiment here (although it is worth noting that the film *is* narrated, voice-over, by Quentin II, so that the question arises: if they were willing to allow one first-person narrator, why not have three or four, as in the much earlier *Citizen Kane*?). What makes Benjy's narrative so difficult to read, however, is not its montage but the fact that it is *words* about wordless experience. Faulkner is continually having to provide indirect clues as to how old Benjy is in a given memory, or what he is seeing. These problems would not arise in a film; the viewer could simply *see* that Benjy was young or old, near a pasture or outside a barn, etc. The logic of Benjy's associations, which would be evident from his cutting from one memory to another, would show how he felt and insure the viewer's realizing that the sequence was subjective.

There is no reason a faithful adaptation of *The Sound and the Fury* could not begin, as the novel does, with a shot of Benjy and his attendant (Luster) moving along the fence of a golf course, with Benjy moaning when the golfer yells "Caddie!" When Benjy gets caught on a fence-nail, and Luster upbraids him, the image could simply cut—as Benjy flashes—to a time when he had gotten caught on a fence-nail and been helped through by Caddy, who had then told him to put his hands in his pockets on account of the cold. To continue the scenario: Benjy now flashes (cuts) to another time he had been kept inside on account of the cold, when what he had wanted was to go outside to meet Caddy on her way home from school. Outside at last, his attendant (Versh) tells him to put his hands in his pockets, but he keeps them out to welcome Caddy. When she gets there, she upbraids Versh for letting Benjy's hands get cold, and rubs them in her own. Stirred by the memory, Benjy begins to moan, and cuts to the present, where Luster yells at him for yelling, then gives him a jimson weed; they go to the fence. Cut to Caddy rubbing Benjy's hands—and so on. By the same token, one could cut from Benjy's section to Quentin's, then to Jason's, and then to a third-person conclusion.

Transferred scene-for-scene, of course, such a film would be too long for commercial release, but that is not an argument against adapting the novel's *techniques*—which are, in any case, primarily visual. It is even arguable that the inherent difficulty of the Benjy section stems from the possibility that *it* is a kind of adaptation: that it was conceived as a visual montage and recast into language. So although it would be difficult and challenging to film this sequence as Faulkner wrote it, it would hardly be impossible, and the result would—*without* oversimplification—be more accessible than the novel. The Ravetches' approach, which is simply to film Benjy's *face*, is entirely inadequate. His stream of consciousness cannot be communicated by an image of the outside of his body; no more can Quentin's memories and conflicts, or the implications of his struggles, be expressed by showing an old alcoholic who whines about his jealousy. All we find out is that he is jealous.

The basic challenge, then, in bringing a novel to the screen, is to translate its words into images—to find a visual way of telling the story. It is not enough simply to show the characters' going through the events the novel is about; the adaptors must show what the story means, how the characters feel, and why the audience is supposed to care about it all. There is nothing inherently wrong with changing the story, if it can be told better that way. A boring film that tells the precise story of an exciting novel is not a "faithful" adaptation. Without being slavish, one can be reasonably faithful to the plot, to the ideas and characters that make the plot interesting, to the techniques that structure the work, or to all of these. Or one can improvise freely, until one has produced not so much an adaptation as a variation. There are numerous examples of the success of both approaches, from Erich von Stroheim's *Greed* on the one hand, to James Whale's *Bride of Frankenstein* on the other. But when all that one retains are the names of the characters and the box-office appeal of the title, or twists scenes so that they not only lose their original meanings but achieve nothing of value on their own, then the adaptation deserves to be called a failure, if not a betrayal. The makers of *The Sound and the Fury* adapted neither Faulkner's story nor his techniques, and made a bad film to boot—not because they were *intimidated* by a classic but because they *distrusted* it. Fortunately, these observations do not apply to most of the other films made from Faulkner's novels; they do, however, suggest the criteria by which those other films should be judged.

3 HOLLYWOOD IN JEFFERSON

Faulkner wrote *Sanctuary* to make money; it was, he said, the most gruesome story he could think of. He is also on record as saying that he wrote screenplays for money. He never got rich from either, but in each case he did good work. Writing for money, to him, seems to have involved not "prostituting his talents" but shortening his sentences: telling the story in such a way that it could be understood in one reading (or viewing). Hawks has defined a good director as "somebody who doesn't annoy you." In his so-called potboilers Faulkner abandons overt metaphysics, montage, and the rhetorically tangled endless sentence. His audiences are not annoyed, then, but it would be entirely off-base to suggest that they are not disturbed, inspired, prodded, entertained, moved.

Sanctuary is a brilliant novel, one of his best. It is the story of two people: Horace Benbow, a middle-aged lawyer on the run from a bitter marriage, and Temple Drake, a college girl who is initiated by rape and bloodshed into a perverse world where she finds herself more than comfortable. Like that of *Absalom, Absalom!*, the Biblical title of this novel is furiously ironic. A sanctuary is a holy place in which to hide. For Benbow, this place is the law; for Temple, a corncrib; for the people of Jefferson, and even for Benbow, the abstract inviolacy of Southern womanhood. As incarnated in Miss Drake, who is raped in her hiding place by an impotent gangster (he uses a corncob), the "temple" of the latter virtue is violated. The courtroom, where one might expect justice, is defiled by Temple's perjury, by the ambition of its officers, and by the failure of Benbow to gauge the horror in which he is involved. There is no holy place, no sanctuary.

The stories of Horace and Temple are interwoven, with the emphasis on Horace. At the beginning of the novel, Horace leaves his wife and goes, let us say, to "hide" with Narcissa, his vain and merciless sister. On the way to Jefferson he comes on Popeye, a thin black-suited bootlegger whose main vehicles of self-expression (besides rape and murder) are matches and cigarettes. Popeye takes him to a still kept by Lee Goodwin at the Old Frenchman Place (a decayed mansion that will, in Faulkner's later novel, *The Hamlet*, help to give the amoral Flem Snopes his boost into Jefferson society). Benbow gets drunk and talks about his marriage, then goes into town. At his sister's he meets Gowan Stevens, the recent graduate of a college where he learned how to drink like a gentleman, but not much else.

Gowan has a heavy date with Temple, the red-haired virgin daughter of Judge Drake. When she repulses his advances (to his surprise, since his introduction to her had been via a lavatory inscription), he takes her to Goodwin's still to get a bottle, wrecking his car in the process. Gowan gets drunk and passes out. Temple is chastised and looked after by Goodwin's common-law wife, Ruby (who is busy with her own sick child). In the morning Gowan, afraid to face Temple, abandons her. Afraid of Popeye and Goodwin but unwilling to walk back to town, Temple hides in a corncrib, guarded by a half-wit boy, Tommy. Popeye shoots Tommy, rapes Temple, and then takes her, unresisting, to Miss Reba's Memphis brothel. When she discovers Popeye's impotence, Temple becomes contemptuous of him. Popeye sets her up with another gangster, Red; he leans over the bed and "whinnies" (cries?) while they make love. When the lovers try to meet on their own, Popeye kills Red.

Meanwhile Lee Goodwin has been arrested for Tommy's murder, and Benbow has taken the case. Through the help of the corrupt and invariably dirty Senator Clarence Snopes, Benbow traces Temple to Miss Reba's, questions Temple (who half-lies), and later subpoenas her. At Goodwin's trial she testifies that Goodwin killed Tommy and raped her. Goodwin is impaled and burned by a self-righteous crowd ("We made him wish we had used a cob"); Temple goes on a European tour with her father; Horace, thoroughly vanquished, goes back to his wife. Then, in the novel's last chapter, Faulkner tells the story of Popeye's life, making him not just human but understandable, and gets him executed for a murder he didn't commit. (In both trials, the wrong-headed juries are out just eight minutes.)

The novel made Faulkner notorious, not for what he showed but for what he suggested. Its narrative method is circuitous and dark; things come clear only in retrospect, and for this indirection are all the more powerful. What is left to the imagination overwhelms it. When *Sanctuary* was bought for the movies, there was no question of telling the story either as Faulkner conceived it or as he told it.

The Story of Temple Drake (1933), as adapted by Oliver H. P. Garrett and Maurine Watkins, directed by Stephen Roberts, and evocatively photographed by Karl Struss, follows the shallows of the novel but avoids its depths. The three things it will not allow, and which are basic to the novel, are impotence, perjury, and failure. Even the rape is presented as somehow appropriate, as Temple's come-uppance for her career as a sexy tease. There is no corncob—consequently no Red and no second murder. There is also no Senator Snopes and no miscarriage of justice, so that the range of the novel's indictment is restricted. What happens is that Temple kills Popeye (re-christened Trigger) and confesses the whole truth at Goodwin's trial. Horace (now Stephen Benbow, vigorous and unmarried) is proud of Temple and will probably marry her.

As Richard Watts, Jr. observed in his review of the film, these changes were "intended only to keep the facts of life and letters from the sensitive reach of Mr. Hays, whose fine sensibilities must be protected in such matters. You and I, however, know that the film . . . is intended as the closest approach that the cinema, considering everything, can make to Faulkner's perverted and sinister narrative."[1] Mr. Hays, however, was not misled, and *The Story of Temple Drake* considerably strengthened the hand of his censorship office. For its period, then, the film was as true as it could feasibly be to the dark side of Faulkner's novel.

Yet even accepting this censoring of the plot, another critic bemoaned Paramount's abandonment of Faulkner's narrative method:

> Reading *Sanctuary* is like watching indistinct objects swim up toward the surface of the water, only to sink before they become quite clear, to sink and swim up again and again to sink. . . . And the sinister is less sinister when spread before one's eyes [in this film] than when half-told, then half-retold and guessed at with difficulty.[2]

Although these remarks are unfair to Karl Struss's moody cinematography, they apply well to both novel and script, and go to the heart of the problem of bringing Faulkner to the screen. The excellence of his work, like that of most fiction, depends on the interplay of story and technique. Where the story is rejected as untellable, and the technique as unmanageable, one has the right to ask just what is left. What is left, in this case, is a good melodrama—a cautionary tale of degeneration and redemption. And although Faulkner hated the film, he evidently felt that the story *was* incomplete without some nod in the direction of redemption, since he wrote a sequel to the story (*Requiem for a Nun*, 1951) in which the temple is reconsecrated.

The gist of that sequel is as follows. To make up for his conduct, Gowan swears off drinking and marries Temple. Temple, however, is nostalgic for Miss Reba's, and hires Nancy Manningoe—one of Reba's ex-employees, "a nigger dopefiend whore"—as nursemaid for her two children. She does this to have someone to talk to. Red's brother shows up, with blackmail on his mind, but instead he and Temple decide to run off together, intending to take with them Temple's infant daughter. To stop them, and to make

Temple aware of the moral implications of her fall, Nancy kills the daughter. For this, she is condemned to death. Gowan's uncle (or perhaps cousin), the lawyer Gavin Stevens, urges Temple to plead with the Governor for Nancy's life, and arranges for Gowan to overhear Temple's confession of indirect responsibility. She has at last rejected perjury, and will be the better for it. Nancy, however, is not reprieved, and goes to her death after attempting to impart to Temple some of her staunch belief in God's righteousness. (Nancy is the "nun" of the title.)

In this context, Temple's story is not so censorable, and the next film of *Sanctuary* (1961), as written by James Poe and directed by Tony Richardson, is as true to its source as one might reasonably hope. The source in this case is Albert Camus' dramatization of *Requiem for a Nun* (which is itself Faulkner's only "play," its three acts broken up by lengthy and eloquent prefaces). The casting is impeccable: Lee Remick as Temple, Bradford Dillman as Gowan, and Odetta as Nancy all bring to their roles a considerable moral intensity, and Richardson's direction is fluid and efficient. The screenplay's most pronounced innovation is evident in the casting of Yves Montand as "Candyman," who is Popeye, Red, and Red's brother all in one. At first this decision sounds disastrous—another Yul-Brynner-as-Jason move—but it turns out to simplify the story gracefully, as does the collapsing of Nancy and Ruby Goodwin into one character.

As James Poe re-invents it, the story begins with Nancy's sentencing, and proceeds to a confrontation between Gowan and Temple. Gowan is still an alcoholic, and their marriage is structured on his refusal to admit that Temple enjoyed herself in the brothel. His uncle—renamed Ira Stevens to avoid confusion—talks Temple into confessing to the Governor, who in this case is her father, Judge Drake. (Gowan is not present.) For the next half hour of screen time, Temple tells the story of *Sanctuary*, with these differences:

After Gowan passes out, Nancy (formerly Ruby) warns Temple not to take the bootleggers lightly. Lee Goodwin is a sex-hungry slob, and "the Candyman—he'll have you crawling on all fours and howling like a dog." Tommy (now "Dogboy," played in a seedy whisper by Strother Martin) escorts Temple to the corncrib—but whereas Popeye kills Tommy, Candyman only slaps Dogboy before going in to rape Temple. Rather than abandoning his date, Gowan is driven off by Goodwin and told that Temple had been picked up by her father. At Miss Reba's, Temple becomes infatuated with her potent Cajun and with alcohol. She likes being "low down," but Candyman wants her to behave like a lady, and never to consider anything like whorish behavior. Temple calls the brothel "a sanctuary of sin and pleasure." As there is no murder, there is no lawyer to track Temple down and no occasion for perjury; Temple is traced through her car, which is wrecked by Candyman and Dogboy during a liquor run. The police find one charred body (Dogboy) and assume it is Candyman. Temple goes home, heartbroken, and lets Gowan talk her into marriage.

Seven years later she finds Nancy in a drug rehabilitation center and hires her. When he finds out who she is, Gowan gets angry. At this point Candyman shows up, and he and Temple plan to run away. Nancy kills the child they plan to take, and Candyman disappears. The Governor understands the meaning of Nancy's action, but refuses to condone the murder of his grandson. Ira takes Temple home, then gives Gowan a lecture on the virtues of facing the truth. Temple and Nancy play their big scene in the death cell, alone. (Faulkner has Gavin/Ira present, explaining everything in his baffled and windy fashion. Poe unquestionably improves the scene, giving Gavin's heaviest lines to Nancy, so that she becomes more tragic and more intelligent than Faulkner allowed her to be, and Richardson improves even the script, by radically shortening and clarifying the dialogue.) Outside the jail, Temple is met by Gowan, who is ready to begin their marriage on the new footing of truth and acceptance. At this point, the film threatens to become a conventional romance, with the deaths of Nancy and the daughter going down as unfortunate events whose value is in their helping to fix a marriage—but Richardson saves the film with one (unscripted) shot. As Temple and Gowan walk off, the camera pulls back to show Nancy in her cell, with her mind on salvation; the wide screen keeps her and the couple both in view (with Nancy in the foreground), and insists on the complexity of this multiple redemption.

There are two ways of evaluating the burden of these changes: dramatically and thematically. To tell the whole story of Temple's fall and rise as Faulkner wrote it, would involve a good deal of repetition: two seductions, two murder trials, two idealistic lawyers, two long-suffering fallen women, two dead or dying children, and so on. *Sanctuary* and *Requiem* are in fact a diptych. The basic story elements of the one are repeated (in a different moral context) in the other. One might guess that Faulkner—dissatisfied with the downbeat *Sanctuary*, as if with a broken leg that had mended badly—had re-broken the leg in the same place to set it again. Within the limits of a two-hour film, the simply *expository* demands of this story would be excessive. So it seems dramatically justifiable to incorporate Ruby into Nancy, Horace into Gavin/Ira, Red and Red's brother into Candyman, and Judge Drake into the Governor. But Lee Goodwin gets lost in the shuffle, and with him Temple's most serious sin. Candyman comes from the same place as the earlier Trigger. Neither *Sanctuary* nor *The Story of Temple Drake* is willing to talk about impotence; each resolves the problem by making the Popeye figure sexually attractive, so that Temple's reasons for staying with him are more conventionally acceptable. Although these condensations are dramatically admirable, then, they raise certain thematic problems.

For one thing, Temple's character is considerably cleaned up. She is not simply perverse, but at worst only lusty and irresponsible. The meaning of the film (which is not far from Faulkner's in *Requiem*) is seen in her deciding to find sanctuary in faith and honesty rather than in sexual/romantic impulse. The problem is that she is presented as somehow always having *known* that honesty is the best policy, with Gowan being the principal evader, and both of them victims of alcohol; everything might have been fine, then, if only Gowan had not felt so guilty and angry, and Candyman not been so attractive. Although Temple acknowledges her own part in these conflicts, they still seem to circle *around* her, as if she were somehow always trying to follow her best impulses. Without a great fall, it is hard to have a great redemption. Thus the film's thematic pussyfooting circles back and becomes a dramatic flaw. Once Temple has been made over in this fashion (as she is in the courtroom climax of the earlier film), there is no point in keeping Popeye; the Candyman will do just fine. By the same token, one never sees Nancy take drugs or turn a trick, and would be hard-pressed to imagine her doing so. With the issue changed from damnation to irresponsibility, this film gives us what Faulkner said but not why he said it.

Poe's script does have the advantage, however, of being markedly less racist and patronizing than *Requiem*—or for that matter, than Faulkner. The primary virtue of many of Faulkner's blacks is their ability to "endure": to bear the burdens of injustice and oppression imposed on them by the whites until their moral strength (and that of the whites who either "endure," as in *Pylon*, or "just don't stop," as in *Intruder*) brings about a millennium of enlightened humanism. This is Dilsey's role, for instance, in the Compson family, as it is Nancy's in *Requiem.* It is all very well to admire fortitude, but another thing entirely to argue that rebellion is inappropriate—and Faulkner does both, with unfortunate results, in his major statement on racial conflict, *Intruder in the Dust.* It is significant that Ben Maddow's script from this novel, like Poe's from *Requiem*, refuses Faulkner's concept of what might be termed "the black man's burden," and achieves through that refusal much of its excellence. In this respect at least, both adaptations improve on their originals.

Between *The Story of Temple Drake* (1933) and *Intruder in the Dust* (1949) no films were made from Faulkner's fiction. (*Today We Live* was released one month before *Temple.*) Hawks didn't see the point of trying to make (or remake) *Sanctuary*, since there was no way to get the original story past the censors; nor did he want to make *Pylon* or *Light in August*, although Faulkner approached him with both. MGM bought *The Unvanquished* but never used it. Faulkner's own treatment of *Absalom, Absalom!* was rejected by Warner's (for reasons that will become clear when that adaptation is discussed in Chapter Five). A screenplay was written by Harry

Behn and Jules Furthman from Faulkner's story, "Honor," but MGM decided not to produce it, perhaps because the plot was sexually risqué. That script was first completed in March, 1933, and rewritten in June of that year, after the release of *The Story of Temple Drake*; it seems likely, then, that the bad notices of the one film doomed the other—and it's a shame, because the Behn/Furthman screenplay (on which Faulkner may also have worked) is very fine. Be that as it may, no studio would touch his fiction; it was not only difficult (and rapidly going out of print), but demonstrably poor box office into the bargain.

Intruder in the Dust, however, was a natural, and the rights were sold to MGM within a month of its publication. Faulkner was so glad of the $50,000 this brought him that he said he had "a right to get drunk and dance in his bare feet." When the director, Clarence Brown, decided to shoot the film on location in Oxford, Mississippi, Faulkner showed him the places he thought would best suit, and even did some uncredited revision on Ben Maddow's script. He left town during much of the filming, however, and was reticent during the première hullabaloo; nevertheless, he thought it was a good picture—as well he might. Brown's direction is lucid, the cinematography by Robert Surtees belongs with the best of his work, Robert J. Kern's editing is sharp and rhythmic, and Juano Hernandez's performance as Lucas Beauchamp is downright brilliant. Taken on its own merits, *Intruder* is the best movie yet made from a Faulkner novel; it is also, coincidentally, the most faithful to its source.

Faulkner's narrative method here, as in *Sanctuary*, is fairly indirect: there is a lot of "half-telling, half-retelling, and guessing with difficulty." In some cases, an event will come clear a hundred pages after it is first mentioned; in others, the implications of a confrontation will be prepared for several chapters, then fall into place with a few lines of dialogue. Maddow decided for the sake of clarity to be consistent in showing an event and afterward (if necessary) explaining what it meant. Thus where both novel and film open with the sheriff's bringing Lucas to the jail, Faulkner is instantly off on a lengthy flashback in the mind of Chick Mallison (the adolescent around whose point of view both novel and film center), so that the reader fully understands why Lucas then asks *Chick* to get him a lawyer; the film, however, shows Lucas's singling Chick out of the hostile crowd and *then* has Chick explain to the lawyer (his uncle—Gavin Stevens again) the history of his relationship with Lucas. On the whole Maddow's method is superior, making for a lot less talk—particularly since it is in the explanatory moralizing of Gavin Stevens that Faulkner hangs himself. (Only in the final scene is Faulkner's explaining-in-advance method better than Maddow's explaining-afterward; there is simply no way to improve on Faulkner's last line.)

It will simplify matters, then, to tell the story of the film rather than of the novel. Lucas Beauchamp, a proud, landowning old black, is arrested for the murder of Vinson Gowrie, a white man. The town of Jefferson is glad of this chance to make Lucas "act like a nigger for once," and looks forward to burning him alive after Vinson is decently buried. Lucas asks Chick to bring his uncle down to the jail. At home, Chick tells Stevens (here called John Gavin Stevens, for no apparent reason) how he had fallen into Lucas's frozen creek several years before; Lucas had dried and fed him, then refused Chick's attempt to pay him. Chick had tried to erase this humiliation by sending Lucas gifts, but Lucas had refused to let the exchange balance out. Thus Chick feels still in his debt, and still resentful. (In the novel, Chick's obligation has already been discharged, so that he approaches Lucas as more of a free agent. This is a significant change, as should soon prove clear.) In the cell, Stevens makes it obvious that he considers Lucas guilty; on the way out, he breaks his pipe (which the actor uses as a symbol of Stevens's professionalism). Lucas therefore asks Chick to clear him, by digging up Vinson's body and proving that he was not shot by Lucas's .41 Colt. Beyond this, Lucas will not volunteer any information—particularly to Stevens, whom he considers "too full of notions." Chick reports the exchange to Stevens and to Miss Eunice Habersham (assertively played by Elizabeth Patterson), an eighty-ish chicken farmer who immediately believes in Lucas's innocence.

As it develops, Eunice and Chick and Aleck Sander (the son of the Mallisons' black maid) go out to the graveyard at midnight and dig up what turns out to be an empty coffin. On the way, they had hidden from a man carrying something on a mule; the "something" turns out to have been Vinson's body. They go to Sheriff Hampton with Stevens, and draw up a plan: Miss Habersham will, by appealing to their chivalric impulses, keep the mob from burning Lucas until the sheriff can unearth the non-body officially. That morning, as they start to dig, they are interrupted by the murdered man's father, the one-armed Nub Gowrie. When he begins to believe them, he has two of his other sons do the shoveling. They then trace the mule tracks to a quicksand, and Nub jumps in for his boy. With difficulty, both are pulled out. In an extremely affecting scene, Nub brushes the crusts of quicksand from the corpse's face, then covers it with his hat. A rifle bullet retrieved from the body implicates Vinson's brother Crawford. At this point Lucas tells Stevens some of what he has been holding back:

Vinson and someone (Lucas will not name Crawford) had been running a lumber business, and Vinson's partner had been stealing his share every night. Both partners knew Lucas had seen one of the thefts. On Saturday (it is now Monday) Lucas had taken his customary walk to the store, carrying his .41 Colt (just like a white man); he had shot at a rabbit and missed. Vinson had encountered him, and was about to beat the name of the thief out of him when he was shot—from a great distance, by someone Lucas never saw. Lucas had been found with a recently-fired pistol, standing near the body.

Stevens and the sheriff lay a trap for Crawford, who has been leading the lynch mob: they make it appear that Lucas has been released and gone home; then Nub and the sheriff wait for him at Lucas's cabin. Crawford fires at the house, then is disarmed by his father. Crawford's guilt is confirmed to the mob by Nub, and Lucas is freed. A week later, Lucas comes to Stevens's office to pay his bill; Stevens charges him $2 for his pipe, then asks why Lucas hadn't confided the truth in the first place. "Would you have believed me?" Lucas asks, and Stevens goes into an angry freeze, clamping on his pipe and starting to read the paper. He looks up, sees Lucas still waiting, and asks what he wants. "My receipt," says Lucas, with an assurance that makes Sidney Poitier look hysterical. As Stevens and Chick watch him walk away, Stevens calls Lucas "the keeper of my conscience." "*Our* conscience, Uncle John," says Chick, and the picture ends.

Again, this outline reveals two kinds of changes, dramatic and thematic, but in this case both are for the better. The plot has been simplified by leaving out a second murder (Crawford also kills Jake Montgomery, to whom he had been selling the stolen lumber and who had been trying to blackmail him; the first time Vinson's grave is opened, Jake's body is found in it) and by changing Crawford's weapon from a Luger to a rifle so that Lucas can be presented as not having seen Vinson's killer. (In the novel Crawford tricks Lucas into shooting at a stump before himself shooting Vinson; later, Crawford kills himself in prison with his own pistol, since his murdering his brother has so cut him off from humanity that the townsfolk will not even give him the dignity of a lynching.) There are other minor changes which tend to heighten the drama of the film, such as having Nub reveal Crawford's guilt in public, but the most important ones are in the final scenes.

The way Faulkner has it, Stevens and Chick discuss for two chapters the implications of the story; then Lucas comes to the office on Saturday, *without* his customary pistol (which he has, in the film) and settles his account: $2 to replace one of Stevens's pens. "My receipt" is the last line of the novel, and there is no "Would you have believed me"—thus no spelling-out of the long way Stevens yet has to go. Faulkner's intention in these two chapters is to assert that the South can take care of itself —that any Northern intervention would not only rob the South of its right to "expiate and abolish" the injustices it has created, but also in some way make the rights "Sambo" [sic] would win not worth having "because by that time divided we may have lost America." This is the significance of Chick's deciding to help Lucas apart from any sense of indebtedness, and of the county's innocents (women and children) setting straight a mystery that ought to have—in the eyes of any "outsider" or even any "Southerner"—led directly to a lynching. The novel is a working-out of the way Faulkner felt racial conflicts ought to be solved, with Lucas holding his ground ("enduring") and the community solving its problems on its own.

Maddow reduces this harangue to a short scene between Stevens and Chick. As the lynch mob drives away, Chick says they're running for three reasons: so they won't have to admit they're wrong, so they won't have to burn Crawford, and so they won't have to face Lucas. Stevens says it's worst than that—they're running from themselves. At this point Miss Habersham drives by and says, "If you ever get in trouble again, let me know." "See," says Stevens, "*we* were in trouble, not Lucas Beauchamp." Chick looks at him hard, and begins to understand. This is followed by the payment scene, through which Lucas keeps the symbols of his assertion: the pistol and the question. Then the point is reinforced in the final exchange on conscience. By dispensing with the issues of Northern intervention and of endurance, these scenes change the meaning of the novel without undermining its value. In both novel and film, Chick is educated out of his satisfaction that Lucas is going to be made to act like a nigger for once, Stevens is knocked out of his complacent pre-judgments, and Lucas keeps his hold on his pride. Nor is there any sense, in novel or film, that the South needs any outside help. The difference arises simply from Maddow's having had the good sense to shut Stevens up and to let the heart of the story tell itself. One can hope that this was a decision with which Faulkner agreed. (The burden of Faulkner's few dialogue revisions was to downplay Stevens's political infallibility. Lucas's "Would you have believed me?" for instance, is probably Faulkner's insertion.)

It is worth noting at this point that even with Poe's and Maddow's down-playing of the "endurance" motif, the blacks in these films do not lapse into Hollywood clichés. (The exception is Aleck Sander, who is *supposed* to be a cliché.) They remain Faulknerian in their obstinate strength. The Ravetches' Dilsey is just a *Gone with the Wind* mammy—another indication of their failure to keep pace with Faulkner—but Odetta and Juano Hernandez (both in their first roles) come into two of the most complexly assertive parts Hollywood has yet offered to black actors. In this context it should not be surprising that the compromise between Faulkner and Walt Disneyism that the Ravetches worked out for Rupert Crosse in *The Reivers* won him an Academy Award nomination—the first time a black had ever been nominated for best supporting actor.

The next Faulkner novel to be filmed was *Pylon*, and even as one of his least successful works it demands something better than *The Tarnished Angels* (1957). *Pylon* is an anguished and fragmented but hard look at the heroic—the story of a cadaverous drunken reporter's involvement with an air-circus pilot, a parachutist, the woman they share, and their son, who was named after a throw of the dice. The reporter is a cross between Faulkner himself and T. S. Eliot's J. Alfred Prufrock, just as the airfield is a cross between a three-dimensional advertisement and "The Waste Land" out of which its foundations were dredged. The novel is pretentious and overwritten, baffled by its own material, hopeless; yet there is no way to understand Faulkner without seeing him with his guard down—as he is here, in perhaps his most personal book. As it is the story of this reporter's infatuation with what may as well be called tarnished angels, and centers on his utter failure to control or save them, there is little to be said about this film—in which the girl falls for the reporter and is finally saved by him from a fate worse than death (hustling)—beyond that it betrays what little soul or energy the novel could claim in the first place.

Like *Absalom, Absalom!*, which Faulkner was writing at the same time, *Pylon* is a story about trying to tell a story, to get to the heart of someone else's heroic experience. In each novel the mythic adventurer (Thomas Sutpen in *Absalom* and the flyers in *Pylon*) overwhelms the vicarious romantic (Quentin Compson and the reporter, respectively), reducing him to a self-destructive wreck whose only recourse is to express his bafflement in a torturous and compulsive stream of rhetoric. The adventurer's story takes on meaning only through the ghostly romantic's attempt to understand it—in fact, through the intensity of that failure. Simply to film the original adventure, then, although it might make for a good action picture, drastically reduces the scope of the attempt and frankly junks its integrity, its mystery, and its point. The point of *Pylon* is comparable to that of *The Great Gatsby*, in which a privileged eavesdropper comes to understand the "greatness" of a man who is widely considered a fool. The point of *The Tarnished Angels* is that men should accept the love of their loved ones rather than sacrifice them for glory, and that mothers should devote themselves to their children: as if *Gatsby* had resolved itself by having its hero give up gangstering and settle down with a nice girl who would appreciate him.

Basically, the story of *Pylon* is as follows. A nameless reporter covers an airmeet during Mardi Gras. He befriends a mechanic named Jiggs and the child Jiggs is teasing ("Who's your old man today, kid?"). This tease turns out to have been begun by the child's *mother*, Laverne Shumann, who forms a *ménage à trois* with her husband—Roger, a racing pilot—and a parachutist, Jack. The reporter dreams of joining the group in bed, but never says so to Laverne. After Roger crashes his plane, the reporter helps him get a larger, unsafe one from another distinguished pilot, Matt Ord. Ord warns them about the plane, but they insist. During the next race the plane disintegrates in mid-air, and Roger uses the last of his control to crash into a lake that borders the airfield, rather than into the grandstand. With Roger dead, Laverne and Jack go off together, abandoning the child with Roger's parents. The reporter, who has spent most of his time trying to understand his fascination with these people, getting fired and rehired by his editor, and almost indistinguishably drinking and vomiting, writes two accounts of the story for his paper. The first is a sappy meditation on Roger's "Last Pylon" (a pylon is a course-marker); the second is more to the point:

> At midnight last night the search for the body of Roger Shumann, racing pilot who plunged into the lake Saturday p.m., was finally abandoned by a three-place biplane of about eighty horsepower which managed to fly out over the water and return without falling to pieces and dropping [sic] a wreath of flowers into the water approximately three quarters of a mile away from where Shumann's body is generally supposed to be since they were precision pilots and so did not miss the entire lake. Mrs. Shumann departed with her husband and children [Laverne is pregnant with Jack's child] for Ohio, where it is understood that their six year old son will spend an indefinite time with some of his grandparents and where any and all finders of Roger Shumann are kindly requested to forward any and all of same.[3]

This ironic mess is the only way he can deal with the tangles of the situation and his tangled feelings about it. The novel ends with his going out to get drunk.

The basic problem with *The Tarnished Angels* is that its makers preferred the first eulogy, in which Roger is described as flying against "but one competitor . . . Death. . . . And so today a lone aeroplane flew out over the lake on the wings of dawn and circled the spot where Roger Shumann got the Last Checkered Flag," etc. Rock Hudson, as the reporter, does his best with what's left of the character who could have composed—let alone taken seriously—such sentimental garbage, but the most one can say is that he is more complex and interesting than the part as written.

The same can be observed of Dorothy Malone (Laverne), who got her big start from Faulkner and Hawks as the second bookseller in *The Big Sleep*, and was perhaps trying to return the favor by playing this part as if it were serious. The principal literary references in *Pylon* are to Eliot; in *Tarnished Angels*, the heavy book is Willa Cather's *My Ántonia*, which Laverne is made to carry around as a symbol of her longing for—and determination to return to—her lost Midwestern innocence. Such a substitution is entirely typical, as the plot summary below should indicate. (Sirk read Eliot aloud on the set.)

The Tarnished Angels opens with the child's being teased by a man at the circus. The reporter intervenes and meets Roger (Robert Stack), his mechanic Jiggs (Jack Carson), and Laverne. Laverne is lusted after by the ugly, viscous, mercenary Matt Ord (who owns planes but is not a pilot). As in the novel, the flyers have no place to spend the night, so the reporter takes them to his apartment. But here things nose-dive. Laverne looks up from *My Ántonia* to tell the reporter her life story. Jiggs (an impossible combination of Jiggs and Jack) is on the bed with Roger (now a former war hero); Laverne and the reporter sleep—separately, of course—on chair and couch. A flashback reveals that Jiggs and Roger had decided by a dice-throw which of them would marry the pregnant Laverne, but also suggests that Jiggs was only being noble and had not in fact ever slept with her. (By the end of the film, this matter is made definite: Laverne has always been true to Roger, but Jiggs has let the rumors—of which she is totally unaware—proliferate, to satisfy his vanity.) After Roger wrecks his plane, he tells Laverne to sleep with Ord in exchange for the rights to Ord's plane. The reporter stops her from going on this errand and himself makes a deal with Ord, then returns to his own apartment for a heavy kiss scene with Laverne; they are interrupted (in the film's best moment) by a death-masked Mardi Gras reveler, who laughs at them and then leaves. The next day, Roger dies in the lake. (The emphasis here is on the child, who is trying to get out of a carnival air-ride to help his father, who is of course also trapped in a plane. It is a good scene, but there is some unnecessary business with a crowd that rushes onto the landing field, as if the scenarist could not figure out how to indicate that Roger has no crash-alternative between grandstand and lake.) That night, Laverne yells at the reporter for luring her into wanting something more stable than Roger (and there *are* hints of this conflict in the novel), and goes off with Ord so that *someone* will provide for her child. The reporter goes to Ord's place and talks her out of it by making her realize how the rumors about her sex life have already affected the boy. As the film ends, the reporter puts Laverne and the boy on a plane for the wholesome Midwest, loans her his copy of *My Ántonia*, and tells her sometime to return it to him in person. They fly past a pylon (elsewhere described by the loquacious reporter as a "bony finger of death," but now looking more like the Washington Monument) into an innocent sky.

In other words, having deleted the *ménage à trois* and having blessed the reporter's eloquence, screenwriter George Zuckerman had to invent something with which to tarnish his angels, and so came up with Roger's request that Laverne prostitute herself for a plane. The unconventional thus appears only as a threat, to be exorcised. The director, Douglas Sirk, seems to have taken his cue from Josef von Sternberg's *The Blue Angel*—notably a scene in which Professor Rath is interrupted in a love scene with *his* femme fatale by a clown-faced image of fate—and to have attempted to reverse that film's tragic structure. Beyond this rather blatant attempt to imbue the story with a sense of fatality, Sirk has simply made a tough-action, sentimental romance. The creative "intelligence" here is not Sirk's but that of the producer, Albert Zugsmith, who is on record as saying that he read *Pylon* once and set it aside. Clearly Zugsmith's intention was to reassemble the writer, director, and stars of *Written on the Wind*, his hit of the year before, and to do whatever was necessary to *Pylon* to make it fit.

The problem an adaptation of *Pylon* might have posed is this: how do you dramatize something that *doesn't* happen (a romance between the reporter and Laverne, the finding of a successful expression for conflict, etc.)? Zugsmith's answer is, simply: have it happen. How do you deal with the unconventional? Make it go away, then leer. How do you deal with people you don't understand? Treat them as if they were what you do understand. How do you deal with crummy failure? Make it glorious. It is not true that a film could *not* have been made from this novel, no matter how wordy it is; the basic story is sound. The problem seems to have been that it was also adult. What Zugsmith produced is the story of the Shumanns as their child might have liked to imagine it. In fact the one way of reading *The Tarnished Angels* that makes sense to me is as an Oedipal fantasy in the minds of a writer and a producer who were unwilling to let their mothers be Faulkner's Laverne.

The next year, Wald and the Ravetches made *The Long, Hot Summer* from *The Hamlet.* Both works are comedies about sex and money, but Faulkner and the Ravetches laugh at different things. Where the movie builds to a classically comic finish in which the hero gets the girl and all misunderstandings are cleared up, the novel ends with the anti-hero's successfully conning the one intelligent and detached person in town out of a good deal of money, and going on to bigger things. The hero of the film, although named Ben Quick (from a minor character in *The Hamlet*) and played by Paul Newman, *is* modeled after the anti-hero of the novel, Flem—as in phlegm—Snopes, a frog-like creature with eyes "the color of stagnant water," no morals or decency, and no interest in anything but material success. Clearly, more than a flash of Newman's blue eyes was involved in this transformation. Unwilling to let their princess (now Joanne Woodward) marry a genuine frog, the Ravetches set Flem on their golden pillow and kissed him. The result was a dream that the pillow itself might have had, down to the golden stitching.

The Snopeses, an extensive and aggressive family of white-trash climbers, dominate three of Faulkner's novels —*The Hamlet, The Town,* and *The Mansion*—and many of his stories. Whether they turn up as isolated characters (the dirty senator in *Sanctuary*, for example) or as central, tragic villains (Flem in the *Snopes* trilogy), they function the same way: as symbols of an avalanche of degeneracy. The Snopes novels are Faulkner's equivalent of Richard Wagner's opera cycle, *The Ring of the Nibelungs*, with Flem as the chief nasty dwarf who brings down whatever gods, ideals, and heroes are left—with the difference that Flem is also the mansion-builder (Wotan, in *The Ring*) and thus the agent of his own destruction. The Snopes materials with which the Ravetches worked are the masterful story, "Barn Burning," and *The Hamlet* (written in the mid-1930s and published in 1940). The second Snopes novel, *The Town* (1957), was published just over four months before the screenplay for *The Long, Hot Summer* was completed; *The Mansion*, in 1959, was Faulkner's next-to-last novel. The Ravetches worked, then, with an uncompleted saga, and can be forgiven for not seeing where the events of *The Hamlet* and even *The Town* were leading; still, there is ample evidence that they deliberately reversed the value structure of that first volume, turning Faulkner's anti-capitalist black comedy into a Horatio Alger bedtime story, not through misreading but through grafting. As in their next effort, *The Sound and the Fury*, they kept many of Faulkner's scenes and changed their meanings, kept his characters' names but presented stock Hollywood figures. *The Long, Hot Summer* is just the kind of success story *The Hamlet* parodies; but for all that, it's not a bad picture.

"Barn Burning" is the story of a nasty and unkempt tenant farmer, Ab Snopes, whose major interest in life is burning the barns of the people who cross him, and of his two sons: Flem, who helps with the burning, and

Sarty, who at the age of ten warns Ab's newest landlord that his barn is in danger. Going up to the big house to introduce himself, Ab deliberately tracks manure over De Spain's large, valuable rug. When De Spain gives them the rug to clean, Ab's family ruins it; De Spain attaches Ab's crop as reimbursement, but Ab sues him. When Ab does not win the case outright, he goes up to burn the barn. Sarty warns De Spain and runs away.

The Hamlet begins a few years later, as Ab rents a farm in the "hamlet" of Frenchman's Bend. The big man in town is Will Varner, a veterinarian who runs the general store and owns a lot of property, notably a decaying mansion on whose grounds a treasure is rumored to have been hidden during the Civil War (the Old Frenchman Place, from *Sanctuary*). Varner's overweight bachelor son, Jody, clerks in the store, but spends most of his time guarding his sexy sister, Eula (who couldn't care less). When the Varners find out (from V. K. Ratliff, a sewing-machine salesman who drifts in and out of town) just to whom they have rented the farm, they decide as a sort of "fire insurance policy" not to anger or evict Snopes, and eventually hire Flem as a store clerk. With this toehold established, Flem begins buying, loaning at interest, and conning everything in sight. More Snopeses appear out of nowhere and entrench themselves. Although he is impotent (as becomes clear in *The Town*), Flem marries the passively beautiful Eula Varner when she becomes pregnant by another man, on the condition that her father deed him the Old Frenchman Place as part of her dowry. At this point Faulkner shifts his focus to two of Flem's relatives: Ike Snopes, an idiot in love with a cow that belongs to a widowered farmer, Jack Houston—and Mink Snopes, who is imprisoned after shooting Houston over a $3 pasturage fee. (In *The Mansion*, Mink returns to kill Flem, aided by Eula's daughter. It is perhaps worth suggesting here that the description of Houston's death is one of Faulkner's finest achievements.) In the book's final section, Flem salts the Old Frenchman Place with bags of "treasure" and cons Ratliff and two others into buying it. Among the victims is Henry Armstid, who had bought a wild horse from one of Flem's sometime partners (known only as the Texan); he had spent the $5 his wife had painstakingly earned, and the horse had run away (along with all the others sold that day). His wife had sued Flem for the money, and lost her case. This second fleecing by Flem unbalances Armstid completely, and the novel ends with Flem's going out of his way to look at the madman still shoveling for "treasure"; he spits over the wheel of the wagon into which he has piled Eula and all his goods, and drives off for Jefferson, having used up Frenchman's Bend.

The Long, Hot Summer tells the story of Flem as if he were Sarty, and christens the combination Ben Quick. Quick's problem is that everyone associates him with his father, a notorious barn-burner. He is, it develops, nothing of the kind, but the town's abuse has hardened him to the point that he trusts only money and his own good looks—which, considering he's played by Paul Newman, is not a bad bet. The film opens with the first trial scene in "Barn Burning," with Quick talking like Ab but feeling like Sarty. Thrown out of that town, he heads for Frenchman's Bend (updated to the 1950s), where he rents a farm from the Varners, works his way up to store clerk, and by the end of the film marries the boss's daughter—but she is no Eula.

Will Varner, played with flamboyant relish by Orson Welles (who was about to grapple with *The Tarnished*

Angels' Albert Zugsmith over *Touch of Evil*), has two children. His son Jody (played by Anthony Franciosa) is a disappointment to Varner; all Jody wants to do is make love to his wife Eula (Lee Remick). Jody is soon outclassed by the aggressive Quick, whom Varner would evidently have preferred as a son. Varner's daughter Clara (Joanne Woodward) is a sexually frustrated schoolteacher; she has been waiting for years for Alan Stewart, a nice-guy aristocrat, to propose to her. Although Eula's name is used, then, she appears nowhere in the picture; the Lee Remick figure is far more intelligent and lively (and stereotyped) than Faulkner's latter-day Helen.

Two drastically altered scenes are representative of the Ravetches' intent here. When Quick goes to Varner's house to introduce himself, he deliberately tracks mud on a small rug. Clara brings the rug for Quick to clean, and it is never mentioned again—the point of the scene being simply to get Clara and Quick into their sparring. Quick tells her that the rug is a false issue, that *he* is what "riles" her. Later, Varner agrees to let Quick clerk in the store if he will first auction off some wild horses for him. Quick sells the horses, which all run off (without causing much damage; in the novel, several people get hurt). Something clicks in Varner's head, and he decides Quick is the "big stud horse" for Clara. In the second scene I want to discuss, then, Henry Armstid's sweet gray-haired wife (in the novel she is young, calm, and bitter) comes to the store where Quick is now working, and asks him for the return of the $30 paid for the horse. Quick gives it to her immediately, explaining to the frantic Jody that it's "good business." It will be remembered that in *The Hamlet* Mrs. Armstid had had to sue Flem for her money, and had lost, and that Flem had gone on to ruin what was left of her husband. What this change reveals, then, is a different *philosophy of business.* Faulkner is amused and horrified at the march of Snopesism—at the way the old order of trust, good will, neighborliness, ease, and at least a passing interest in morality falls prey to (and is replaced by) the bourgeois cult of money and social status. Granted that Quick's motive here is not sentiment but deferred profit, the fact remains that the gesture would be entirely beyond Flem. The Ravetches evidently feel that "business" can be conducted well—that self-interest can be enlightened—and so go on to reward Quick for his resourcefulness as well as his under-it-all goodness. (The result is not unlike what you might get if you adapted *Oedipus Rex* for *Father Knows Best.*)

The Ravetches wrap up the story in this fashion: Jody ambushes Quick, who is on his way back from some unsuccessful courting; he wants to kill Quick for taking his place in the world. Quick saves his skin (an honorable motive) by offering Jody the Frenchman Place and its treasure. Jody is delighted at the prospect of thus getting enough money to leave his father, and buys the place after Quick leads him to a (planted) bag of coins. Varner finds Jody digging and points out the coins' recent minting date. After a runaround over Clara's non-engagement to Alan Stewart, Varner throws Clara and Quick together, then goes back to his barn to check on a foaling mare, observing that he's "glad something around here's getting born." Jody locks him in the barn and sets fire to it, then changes his mind—all of which brings father and son closer together, but sets a lynch mob after Quick, the notorious barn-burner. Clara saves Quick, who is "not in a running mood." In her car, he tells Clara that he *hates* fires, that his old man was the arsonist, and that he hasn't seen him since he blew the whistle on Ab when he was ten. Clara, who has likewise rejected *her* unpleasant father, responds that "people are kinder than you think, if you just tell them." The crowd catches up with them, but Varner intervenes, saying he started the fire himself with a cigar. From here the film moves to a most unSnopes-like conclusion, in which Quick lectures Varner on the ethics of dealing ("We started out playing a horseflesh game . . . [but] now we've left horses and gotten around to *people*, and that's something different") before he gets landed by Clara. Jody and Eula are happy again, and even Varner decides to marry his longtime mistress (in the novel, both he and the mistress are married to others already). On the prospect of a triple coupling, with no hard feelings, they all settle down for the night, and the picture ends.

The title was changed from *The Hamlet* to avoid confusion with *Hamlet*, but the change was in any case apt. The film's emphasis is not on the village Flem swallows but on heat: the heat of burning barns and of sexual desire. In the best Victorian tradition, the hero gets money and a good name along with the girl. As in *The Sound and the Fury*, the Ravetches (and Jerry Wald and Martin Ritt) are praising the status quo, which includes capitalist success, male aggression, female self-respect (Clara has many of the same lines as Quentin II, but they fit better here), female domesticity, and the unshakeable value of "getting things out in the open." Most problems are caused by misunderstanding, and the ones that aren't can usually be resolved by a little head-on conflict. None of this, of course, has much to do with Faulkner—but taken on its own merits, the story is coherent, the acting is glamorous but convincing, and the direction is fairly efficient. In contrast to *The Tarnished Angels* (which is, if anything, *more* faithful to its novel) *The Long, Hot Summer* manages to defend convention without becoming obnoxious or pretentious; in contrast to *The Sound and the Fury* it has a story that does not eat itself up with (Hollywood-induced) contradictions. It will never satisfy an admirer of *The Hamlet*, but at least it provides "Barn Burning" with a happy and not absolutely impossible conclusion.

That left *The Reivers: A Reminiscence*, Faulkner's last novel. This time Irving Ravetch acted as his own producer and chose a novel that could be filmed without drastic revision. He and Harriet Frank, Jr. came up at last with a script that reflected their love of Faulkner, and into which their conventional prejudices could fit without too much tinkering. At its worst, *The Reivers* (1969) is like a Disney live-action film, or an extended episode of *The Waltons*; at its best, it is exciting, moving, and visually beautiful.

In *The Reivers*, the old order is ransacked by the advent of the automobile; predictably, the Ravetches celebrate the newcomer's success, as they had Ben Quick's, where Faulkner is less enthusiastic. Faulkner dramatizes the differences between a late-nineteenth century culture of gentlemen on horses and a mid-twentieth century automobile-dependent, overpopulated, and morally neutral urban society through a very simple narrative device: the narrator, Lucius Priest, tells his grandchild in 1961 the story of an excursion he had taken as an eleven-year-old boy in 1905, and of his relations with his own grandfather (Boss Priest), who is a contemporary of Colonel Sartoris and whose attitudes were formed during Reconstruction. The span of reference is one hundred years, or five generations, during the last two of which the technologists have, as Joni Mitchell puts it, "paved paradise and put up a parking lot"; even the seasons have been conquered, and man is at the point of reproducing his kind into oblivion. The act of "reminiscence," then, is partly a search for values. And although the Ravetches and their director, Mark Rydell, follow Faulkner in making 1905 look clean and beautiful, they stop short of suggesting that the equally beautiful yellow automobile will be the decisive force in changing that landscape for the worse. So the voice of old Lucius (read by Burgess Meredith) tells the *movie* audience what 1905 was like, without mentioning the present. The filmmakers do follow Faulkner consistently, however, in paralleling the saga of the automobile's intrusion on a horseflesh economy with the story of Lucius's loss of "innocence"—his learning to lie, to rebel, and to compromise—with the significant difference that they believe there *is* such a thing as childhood innocence, where Faulkner asserts more realistically that children are neither innocent nor ignorant, but only have different appetites and abilities from those of adults.

In the novel, then, Lucius is a good deal smarter than Boon Hogganbeck, a family employee who is under the misapprehension that he has to *seduce* Lucius into riding off with him to Memphis in Boss Priest's new automobile. Faulkner's Boon "was tough, faithful, brave, and completely unreliable; he was six feet four inches tall and weighed 240 pounds and had the mentality of a child; over a year ago Father had already begun to say that at any moment now I would outgrow him."[4] In the film Boon is played by Steve McQueen; his adolescent perkiness is attractive, but there is no getting around the fact that he isn't the part-Chickasaw Boon as much as he is McQueen. The major alteration in his character is that McQueen's Boon acts not like a big kid but like a big brother, and approaches Lucius with the intention of helping him to grow up. Lucius, as played by Mitch Vogel, responds with a great deal of freckled intensity, but remains more a child of Hollywood than of Faulkner. Ned McCaslin, the family coachman (Rupert Crosse), is transformed along similar lines. Where Faulkner has the joyriding car thieves (reivers) discover that Ned has stowed away with them by smelling the effects of his inability to remain continent while hiding under a tarp in the back seat, the Ravetches have Ned announce himself by singing "Camptown Races." Faulkner's Ned plays a game with whites, making himself out as a latter-day Uncle Remus to delude those he doesn't trust, but revealing his calm intelligence when it suits him; he is also married, but not above courting Minnie, a black maid in Miss Reba's Memphis brothel. The Ravetches' Ned is unmarried (and Minnie is virtually dropped from the film), racially-conscious, impulsive, and lots of fun. It is interesting that Faulkner's Ned is much more crafty and secretive than the film allows. In the novel, for instance, Ned is presented as having had for some time a secret way to make obstinate mules and horses perform as he wishes (he lures them with a sardine), so that his staking his and Boon's jobs and futures (and the car) on a horse race is not an outlandish plan; in the film, Ned is over a barrel until he discovers at the last moment—while eating a sardine sandwich—a way to make the horse win. The burden of such changes is that while Ned retains much of his attractive assertiveness and political acumen, he loses a lot of his gutsy intelligence and emerges as a more slapstick figure. It is, as I suggested above, a compromise between Faulkner and Walt Disney; the same can be observed of the film's Lucius and particularly of Corrie (played by Sharon Farrell), Boon's mistress and Miss Reba's star employee.

After Boon drives to the brothel, he leaves Ned to his own devices and introduces Lucius to Corrie and her nephew, Otis (who is far more obnoxious in the novel). Corrie is sweet, short, blonde, and sentimental—an essentially homey type who has taken her job as a way of husband-hunting. In the novel, however, she is big and dark—"just right for serenity" and acutely aware of her fall. When Otis tells Lucius what kind of place they are staying in, and explains Corrie's occupation, Lucius fights him, and the adults intervene. (In the novel Otis has gone on to boast how he used to augment his own income by renting access to a peephole to "brutal and shameless men who paid their pennies to watch her defenseless and undefended and unavenged degradation," and it is the image of these men, along with Otis, that Lucius is attacking.) Corrie tucks Lucius in after bandaging his knife-wound, and he suggests that she'd make a good nurse. She is impressed that a male would fight for her instead of over her, and agrees to stop whoring. This upsets Boon, who is even more upset when he finds Ned has swapped the car for a horse that won't run, and made arrangements to win the car back in a horse race.

With Corrie and the horse, the trio set off for the nearby town of Parsham, where they meet Uncle Possum (Juano Hernandez) and a gross deputy sheriff, Butch Lovemaiden (Clifton James); Possum puts Lucius up for the night, while Butch takes the others to jail, then releases them in exchange for Corrie's favors. Boon hits Corrie (and Butch, in the novel), and Lucius refuses to ride the horse in the race until he realizes that Boss might lose the car if he doesn't; there is also a stock big-brother weeper between Boon and Lucius, and another with Lucius and Corrie. (None of this happens in the novel, but is thrown in to dramatize the attractions of the car and the difficulty of growing up; Faulkner's Lucius never threatens to quit, and Boon is in jail at the time.) After a series of races, which Lucius wins (he wins two out of two in the film, two out of four in the novel), Boss shows up and takes them all home. Boss (Will Geer, last represented in Faulkner films as Sheriff Hampton in *Intruder*) gives Lucius a lecture that is straight out of the book, and Boon marries Corrie. The Hogganbecks name their child after Lucius. But where the novel ends with Corrie's presenting the baby to Lucius and telling him its name (in 1906), the film ends with the prospect of this naming (in 1905) and the merry trio of Ned, Boon, and Lucius play-driving in the car, from which Boss Priest has removed the wheels.

On the whole, *The Reivers* is quite faithful to its source; most of its variations are in the interest of simplifying the plot. It is not as cleaned-up as Richardson's *Sanctuary*, because there is less to clean, but the character changes are still significant, as are the shifts in perspective on the automobile and on the psychology of childhood. Although it is the best one could expect from the Ravetches, then, it is not the best one could demand of the film industry in general—nor are any of these films, with the notable exceptions of *Intruder in the Dust* and a more recent film which is on the verge of financial oblivion: *Tomorrow* (1971).

Tomorrow is one of those low-key, low-budget films that surface in New York for a few weeks in search of an audience and then sink in the face of a couple of bad reviews. Its producers, Paul Roebling and Gilbert Pearlman, have a serious commitment to making good films out of what they consider the "virtually untapped resource of American literature." As their first (and to date only) effort they chose Horton Foote's Playhouse 90 adaptation of Faulkner's "Tomorrow," which is one of the best of the Gavin Stevens stories. "Tomorrow" concerns Stevens' attempt to discover why a poor cotton-farmer, Jackson Fentry, refused to allow the jury on which he was serving to acquit Stevens' client, Bookwright, of the charge of murder. Bookwright had killed Buck Thorpe—a swaggering, uncouth, and married hillbilly—to stop him from running off with Bookwright's daughter. Stevens and Chick Mallison talk to Fentry's neighbors, and then to Isham Quick (who had found Thorpe's body and also, long ago, overseen a sawmill where Fentry had been caretaker). What they find is that Fentry had despaired of ever getting together enough money to marry and have a son, and had left his father's farm for a paying job at Ben Quick's sawmill near Frenchman's Bend. An exhausted, pregnant woman had shown up there one day, given birth to a son, and then—at Fentry's insistence, and realizing she was dying—married Fentry so that someone would take care of the child (the problem being that she is already married). Having gotten all he might ever have wanted from a woman, Fentry took the boy and returned to his farm, where he raised him for five years. Eventually, however, the mother's relatives tracked him down and claimed the boy, intending to raise him as one of their own—as a Thorpe. Perhaps fifteen years later, Fentry ran across his "son"—now Buck Thorpe—but did not speak to him, only watched him out of the corner of his love. As Stevens puts it together: "The lowly and invincible of the earth—to endure and endure and then endure, tomorrow and tomorrow and tomorrow. Of course he wasn't going to vote Bookwright free."[5]

Foote's play and screenplay both concerned themselves

with the page or two in the story that describe Fentry's encounter with the dying woman. The director, Joseph Anthony, felt that this ought to remain the focus of the film. The plot of *Tomorrow*, then, while it works its way around to Stevens (renamed Douglas, for some reason) and Bookwright, is mainly concerned with the long, slow growth of intimacy between Fentry (played brilliantly by Robert Duvall) and the woman, Sarah (in an Oscar-quality performance by Olga Bellin), over the months they share in the dormant sawmill. Fentry is portrayed as wanting to "save" Sarah, to help her want to live; but he discovers at her death that by the time he found her she was "all wore out." He decides to raise the boy, then, as an extension of his commitment to *her*. While the sexual politics of this shift are in many ways preferable to Faulkner's—and one could hardly regret Bellin's eloquent and unsentimental delivery of the role Foote created for her—it is unfortunate that the relationship between Fentry and his "son" is so hurriedly summarized, and that Faulkner's involuted structure of plot-revelation is downplayed in the interest of dramatic "clarity."

With these reservations stated, however, one can hardly fail to praise the film on its own terms. *Tomorrow* is simply one of the best independent productions in the recent history of American narrative film. Alan Green's black-and-white cinematography, at Roebling's insistence, is closely patterned after Walker Evans's work in James Agee's *Let Us Now Praise Famous Men*: one can practically chart the grain in each plank of the sawmill's walls. Both lighting and composition are rigorous, formal, and tender—studies in the eloquence of the simple. Duvall, Bellin, Sudie Bond, and the rest of the actors are perfectly in tone with the mood and form of the image, and Reva Schlesinger's editing balances the speed of the opening and closing sequences (which show the killing, the courtroom, the growth of the boy, the fight over his custody, and the lawyer's response to it all) and the long, slow scenes in the sawmill with masterful control. Irwin Stahl's guitar-and-concertina score—a brilliant set of variations on the folk songs of the period—suits the Mississippi locations and even the faces of the minor players, who were recruited from the local citizenry. If *Tomorrow* and *Intruder* prove anything besides that the Gavin Stevens stories have so far made the best Faulkner films (perhaps because they fit into the pre-existing genre of the courtroom drama), it is that Faulkner's work demands to be shot in the settings that inspired it—that Hollywood does better in "Jefferson" than on its own back lots. With *Tomorrow* and *Intruder* excepted, then, the following conclusions seem just.

Faulkner is a great novelist, but these are not great films. At best they are competent and interesting, at worst sentimental and pretentious. They indulge to varying extents in the forgivable and often necessary adaptor's tactics of plot-simplification and character-melding, in censorship (which passes in *Temple Drake* but not in *The Tarnished Angels*), in white-washing, in updating, and in theme-changing. Having seen them but not read the novels, the audience would have little respect for Faulkner, little knowledge of him. Most of the producers used Faulkner stories for the box-office value of his name—first as the author of *Sanctuary* and later as Nobel laureate—but changed his stories to fit their own preconceptions of the South and of the audience. This is all the more upsetting because Faulkner's narrative techniques (which have been almost totally rejected in these adaptations), complex visions, intriguing story-lines and characters, and adult preoccupations were never *beyond* the reach of the entertainment film, and are quite within the reach of the present-day industry—not to mention the tastes of the modern audience. One might hope that Hollywood (or Paris) would now tackle a cinematic novel like *As I Lay Dying* or *The Wild Palms*, mount an epic production of *Snopes*, or remake *The Sound and the Fury* as it was written, so that the "vast and miscellaneous audience" can get in on some of what it has been denied. It is quite to the point that Faulkner himself worked under this same kind of box-office pressure when he wrote for Hollywood, and that what he produced has its highs as well as its lows, but that he managed in those better moments to be original, provocative, entertaining, and profound without turning the audiences away. There can be little doubt that *The Road to Glory*, *The Big Sleep*, and *The Southerner* will continue to be well-received long after *The Long, Hot Summer* has fanned itself into an even longer fall.

4 TURNABOUT: FAULKNER'S FILMS

"I'm supposed to say all *that*?"

—Humphrey Bogart, on the set of *To Have and Have Not*

Faulkner went to Hollywood with an idea for Mickey Mouse; he left with the idea for *A Fable*, which he considered his "magnum opus," and which was not. Like most of what Faulkner said about his film career, such a neat oversimplification does not do him—or what he wrote—justice. The received myths about his Hollywood work include: that he was simply a "script doctor," called on to fix an occasional scene in screenplays that were primarily the work of other writers; that he did it all for money, counting down the days till payday and drinking himself blind whenever a script was finished; that he took film work seriously, but decided at last that he had no talent for it; and that the screen credits he received were rarely earned. At one time or another, each of these statements applied, but taken in a lump they are misleading.[1] Many of the forty-eight films Faulkner wrote were entirely his own creations; eighteen reached the screen in one way or another, and several of those are classics.[2] At least three of the unproduced scripts—*War Birds, Dreadful Hollow*, and *Stallion Road*—are models of an intense professionalism. From the first he showed a pronounced talent for screenwriting; what he *had* little talent for was getting along with loud extroverts, especially producers. Clearly he had little respect for Darryl F. Zanuck at 20th Century-Fox; clearly he disliked working at Warner Brothers; clearly he was frustrated when scripts he had worked on for weeks were attacked and shelved. On the whole he saw fiction as his main career, and came to resent the time that Warner's in particular drained from his "serious" work, just as he resented the *need* to make money by screenwriting, the need to take orders from people he did not respect. His best work, accordingly, was done for the men he respected: Hawks, Renoir, and himself.

By the time he signed his first Hollywood contract, Faulkner had achieved some recognition as a novelist. His 1926 novel, *Soldiers' Pay*, had been well-received; his second novel, *Mosquitoes*, less so. His next novel, *Flags in the Dust*, which contained *in nuce* the whole Yoknapatawpha cycle, had been rejected by a number of publishers until it was cut and rearranged into *Sartoris* by Faulkner and his New York agent. (The *Sartoris* experience appears to have been decisive, for it was during this enforced revising that Faulkner began to write *The Sound and the Fury*, a novel that he expected would please no one. He learned, that is, not "how to write for publication," but how to write in spite of the demands of businessmen. Like most experimenters, he was his own best first audience. When he had to collaborate in Hollywood, the quality of his achievement varied with the gentlemanliness of the people he worked with, and the tactfulness of their suggestions.) When he visited New York in 1931, he found himself praised as the author of *The Sound and the Fury* and *As I Lay Dying*, and nearly infamous as the author of *Sanctuary*. His stories were finding good markets, and he was welcome at parties. At one of these gatherings he ran into Tallulah Bankhead, who suggested he write her a picture. The idea of such easy money appealed to him, and he asked his agent to land him a Hollywood contract. (His letters home indicate that he immediately began writing a screenplay, perhaps for *Sanctuary*, but no manuscript seems to be extant; I have followed Blotner in assuming that what Faulkner worked on in New York was an early version of *The College Widow*.) On May 7, 1932, he reported to MGM for six-weeks' work.

He had an idea, he said, for Mickey Mouse; the only films he watched, he said, were Disneys and newsreels. He was assigned to a Wallace Beery vehicle, *Flesh*, and taken to a projection room. He left after a few minutes, saying there was no point in seeing the whole film—he "knew how it would turn out." Then he hid out in Death Valley for a week. By May 24 he had settled down to writing films.

There is no point in disputing the truth of this anecdote—only its interpretation. As a child, Faulkner went to the movies regularly. His admiration for D. W. Griffith's *The Birth of a Nation* suggests that he knew about more than Mickey Mouse, just as his retreat from the screening room suggests more than that he was contemptuous of Wallace Beery. What he was, was *nervous*: afraid he would do a bad job, and alienated by the rich and busy city.[3] When he came back, he wrote four treatments in a week—one of them for Beery.

A *treatment* is the preliminary outline for a film, and as such resembles the synopsis of a play. It is usually broken into master scenes, with key lines of dialogue and major characters mapped out. A treatment can be an original story, or an adaptation of a property owned by the studio. If it is accepted by a director or producer, the author (or some other author entirely) is assigned to expand the treatment into a full-length *temporary screenplay*. After story conferences and revisions, a *final screenplay* is approved; this final version, or *shooting script*, is often revised by the director (and sometimes by the actors), and is subject to further condensation and rearrangement by the film editor. Because so many people work on a script, at so many levels and with such different interests, it is difficult to argue back from the *release version* of a film in search of the contributions of a particular author. This discussion of Faulkner's career as a screenwriter, then, centers on the level of script-generation at which it can be established that Faulkner worked, whether on his own or in direct collaboration with others. In the case of his early treatments for MGM, none of which were approved for expansion into temporary screenplays (let alone produced), it is easy to see what Faulkner knew about film—what kinds of plots and techniques struck him as best suited to the medium and to its businessmen—since he worked on his own and, in most cases, from original stories.

His first treatment, *Manservant* (from his own story, "Love"), is no longer in the MGM files.[4] His second, *The College Widow*, introduces two themes that recur in many of his scripts: the definition of a character through his attitude toward honor, and the moral isolation that goes with cowardice and irresponsibility. (If this sounds like a thematic overview of Howard Hawks, one can only be struck by the temperamental complementarity of the two men; they had not yet met.) The heroine, Mary Lee Blair, is the daughter of a professor in a college town. Her fiancé, Robert, has a close friend, Raymond. When Raymond steals some papers from the professor's desk, Robert takes the blame to save his friend. "Mary Lee has not enough character to stick to Robert," and their engagement is broken. She returns to her college-boy flirtations. Later, Mary Lee finds herself attracted to a dark, violent stranger (as Temple is, in *Sanctuary*). After they have an affair, her desire turns to terror; she marries Robert, but the stranger pursues her (an anticipation of *Requiem for a Nun*). When he breaks into the house, Robert kills him; Mary Lee has a miscarriage and insists on divorcing Robert, who remarries. Back in her home town, Mary Lee becomes a hanger-on at college dances; her sexual notoriety disgraces her father, to the point that she has to leave town if he is to keep his position. The treatment ends with Mary Lee, "the companion of middle-aged men at night clubs and such," proposing a toast to Robert's second wife (who does not see her): "To the mother of my son!"

The College Widow, which is presumably the vehicle Faulkner wrote for Tallulah Bankhead, was dismissed by the producers as another *Sanctuary*, too hot to handle. In his next treatment, *Absolution*, Faulkner turned to the apparently safer topic of love between men. Like *The College Widow* it is set in a "small Southern town," until the scene changes to wartime France. Like many of Faulkner's novels, *Absolution* shows how a lifelong obsession can originate in an unforgettable childhood incident (Caddy's muddying her drawers, for instance, or Sutpen's being turned away by the "monkey nigger"); like many of Hawks's films it explores the themes of honor, love, and male bonding in the context of an organized professional effort—in this case, the First World War.

As the story begins, John (lower-class, stolid) and Corwin (upper-class, flashy) are "inseparable companions," aged twelve. One day they have a fight on the school playground: Corwin snatches a hair-ribbon from Evelyn, who cries; John wins the ribbon back and gives it to her. The boys become enemies; "both are now interested in the girl because she was the thing which divided them." Later, John becomes a thug, and Evelyn and Corwin become lovers. The men meet again in France, where John is commander of a squadron of planes and Corwin is a flight cadet. Through an extremely complex series of exchanges, Corwin forces John to kill him. After the war, John visits Evelyn, whom he has worshipped all this time. He is shocked to discover not only that she and Corwin had slept together without any intention of marrying, but also that she was relieved at Corwin's death. He discovers that "he gave up the friend he loved for a woman who was not worth it—finally killed that friend with his own hand for her sake." To seek absolution, he returns to France. He stands by Corwin's grave and draws his pistol.

Neither of these treatments is a literary masterpiece—neither was written for publication. Both, however, are thematically complex and dramatically energetic. The second echoes *Sartoris* as the first does *Sanctuary*, and both are recognizably Faulknerian in tone, setting, and moral dynamic. His next treatment, *Flying the Mail,* was a revision of an existing treatment by Ralph Graves and

Bernard Fineman—a vehicle for Wallace Beery, Marie Dressler, and Robert Montgomery. The Wallace Beery figure (Wally) is an old-fashioned pilot with a hard-headed, nagging, devoted mistress (Min), a close friend and fellow aviator (Johnson), and two children: a daughter ("the girl") and a surrogate son (Bob). Wally has raised Bob from childhood, teaching him everything he knows about flying (Bob had stowed away on Wally's plane during a "record flight"), and spending the rest of his time fleeing his alimony-hungry ex-wife. When America enters the war, Bob enlists but Wally is rejected as unfit. "Wally realizes only now that he is about to lose the boy whom he has raised and loved as his own. . . . Each is ashamed to let the other see that he is loved and will be missed." After the war, Bob and Wally become mail flyers. At one point Bob, who has led a promiscuous life, meets a girl (Wally's daughter) on a train; she is the first woman to resist his advances, and he promptly becomes fascinated by her. When he finds out who she is, they have an exchange that echoes the Dalton Ames episode of *The Sound and the Fury*:

> The girl, "Do you want me to be your sister?" Bob moves suddenly toward her. He is quite serious. Bob, "Say that again." They are both moved.

The girl, like Mary Lee Blair, is on the run from a man she once lived with (Al), but of whom she has become afraid. She and Bob fall in love, but she refuses to tell him about her past. The key scene in the treatment takes place while Bob, Wally, Min, Mrs. Johnson, and the girl are waiting for Johnson to land a mail flight in dense fog. Overwhelmed by her feelings, the girl runs off and gets lost. "The fog becomes a symbol of that which separates them. At last they find one another in the fog. It is as though they had found each other at last, in some place beyond the world and life." Then Johnson's plane crashes and burns. In spite of the girl's protests, Bob loads the mail onto another plane and takes off; sorting the remaining mail, the girl finds a threatening letter from Al, addressed to herself. She goes to Min for advice; Min says, "Look at me and Wally, do you think I have told him all I ever done?" (This is a leap forward in candor for Beery vehicles.) After a series of misunderstandings, fights, and reconciliations, Bob marries the girl and Wally marries Min. All these relationships develop in parallel with a series of advances in aviation. Although the script includes no shot breakdowns, it is clear that by the end of his first week at MGM Faulkner had learned how to construct a linear, visual narrative, and felt free to work with themes that interested *him*: notably those of aviation, promiscuity, and sublimated incest.

His six-week contract was renewed at the insistence of Howard Hawks, who had read Faulkner's story "Turn About" in the *Saturday Evening Post* and wanted him to adapt it himself. It was a straightforward story about an American pilot (Bogard) and his friend (McGinnis), who find a drunken English sailor (Claude Hope) trying to sleep in the middle of a Paris street. Claude is doing this, he explains, because his boat is stored *under* the wharf at night, and he has nowhere else to go. Assuming that Claude is a shirker, Bogard and McGinnis take him up in their bomber to "show him some war." Claude proves to be a competent gunner, and congratulates the Americans for flying half the mission—and even landing—with an incompletely released bomb hanging from one of the wings. (The pilots, of course, were unaware of the bomb.) Turnabout being fair play, Claude takes Bogard on his boat and shows *him* some war. The boat, manned by Claude and his friend (Ronnie Boyce-Smith), ejects torpedoes from its rear, then—with luck—gets out of their way. Bogard is impressed and has a case of Scotch delivered to Claude in the street; he tells the messenger to look for "a child about six feet long." Later, Bogard reads that Claude and Ronnie have been lost in action, and himself makes a daring raid on an ammunition depot, then goes on to bomb the enemy's headquarters; his only regret is that "all the generals, the admirals, the presidents and the kings—theirs, ours—all of them" were not there to be destroyed.

Hawks had been following Faulkner's work since *Soldiers' Pay*. He had considered adapting *Sanctuary* (as discussed above), but felt there was no point in trying to get it past the censors. He now told Faulkner how he wanted "Turn About" to be done, and Faulkner said he could write it in five days. At that point Hawks offered him a drink. The two men woke up in a motel room in Culver City the next morning; Faulkner was fishing cigarette stubs out of a mint julep glass.

Five days later, Hawks brought the script of *Turn About* into the office of Irving Thalberg, to show him what good work "a guy who doesn't know how to write scenarios" could do. "You're not going to muddy it up by changing it?" Thalberg asked, and Hawks said that of course he wasn't. It turned out, however, that MGM needed a vehicle for Joan Crawford, and someone (not Thalberg) decided that this was it. As they had it by this time, *Turn About* was very close to Faulkner's original story, with the significant change that Claude is blinded by an exploding shell during his torpedo run with Bogard.

(This addition was dictated by Hawks, in whose work blindness is a recurring theme, but it should be remembered that the hero of *Soldiers' Pay* had been blinded in combat too.) Faulkner promptly rewrote the entire script —his first full-length screenplay—drawing again on *The Sound and the Fury* for part of his inspiration. He expanded the character of Ronnie Boyce-Smith and gave him a sister, Ann. It seems quite unlikely that (as Blotner suggests) Faulkner was not committed to or interested in this rewrite, since it gave him a chance to expand on his core theme of sublimated incest, and since the screenplay itself is a masterful, moving work. The difficult person to convince was Crawford, who was in tears at the prospect of messing up Hawks's all-male picture. As they sat in the MGM commissary, Hawks told her, "Now look, I don't think you can get out of this. I don't think I can get out of this. We both have contracts. You can make it absolutely miserable unless you accept this well. And if you start taking it miserably, those are the kind of scenes you're going to make." She agreed to do her best—and did. She even insisted, in the spirit of the thing, that Faulkner write her the same kind of clipped, unemotional dialogue he had used in the story and in the male roles of the existing screenplay. By the end of August, Faulkner had completed *Turn About* and signed it—in homage, since Hawks had done none of the writing—with his and Hawks's names.

It was at about this time that Hawks gave Faulkner a crash course in how to write screenplays. He didn't want Faulkner to worry about breaking up the master scenes into shots, but he did insist that the story be told without flashbacks. "The first thing I want is a story," he said; "the next thing I want is character. Then I jump to anything I think is interesting." Faulkner told him that he *liked* the way Hawks made films, and their partnership took shape. From then on, Faulkner did his best to write movies that were clear, powerful, and told in the evolving present.

Turn About opens with one of those childhood-determines-the-rest-of-your-life scenes of which Faulkner was so fond. Ronnie and Ann are playing in a muddy brook, accompanied by Claude—who, as a ward of the Boyce-Smith family, is essentially their brother. Ronnie tells Ann to go away from the water; when she refuses, he shoves her into the brook. Claude and Ronnie fight—as in *Absolution*—but when Claude starts to win, Ann attacks him. A plane flies overhead, and they all stop fighting, enchanted. Ann says that when she grows up she will marry an aviator; Ronnie tells her that she is going to marry Claude. (The connections with the branch episode of *The Sound and the Fury* are striking, with the difference that this Quentin has a "second self" his sister *can* marry. A similar dynamic occurs among Henry, Bon, and Judith in *Absalom, Absalom!*) Later, when Ronnie goes off to school, he tells Claude to take care of Ann, since "girls have no sense." When Claude himself goes off to the same school, he passes her "care" on to Albert, the family servant, and tells Ann not to be a fool like most girls. Her marvelous retort is, "I'm not a fool. I never am." At school, Claude and Ronnie continue to play their favorite game of yelling "Beaver!" whenever they spot a bearded man; Ronnie is always ahead. (As adults, they call "Beaver" when they spot an enemy target.)

Early in the war, their father dies in combat; the mother dies soon afterward. Now in their mid-teens, the three stand on a schoolground, listening to "a faint mutter of gunfire, as though heard from France." Ronnie and

Claude promise to enlist together, when Claude (the younger) is of age. Ann exhorts them: "And then kill them! Kill them!"

At Oxford, Ronnie and Ann meet Bogard. Ann takes an immediate dislike to him for "not being in khaki." Ronnie realizes that she curses Bogard too much and is probably attracted to him. Bogard falls in love with her and enlists, but when he goes to show off his uniform he finds that she and Ronnie have left for France; it is Claude's eighteenth birthday, and all three of them have joined up.

Bogard becomes an ace pilot. One night he finds Claude (whom he has never met) in the street; they go through most of the "turn about" of the original story. By this time Claude and Ann have begun to sleep together; Claude has been drinking a great deal, out of his despair that the war will never end, that there will never be a way to go back to the normal world. Ronnie is not censorious. When Bogard finally encounters and recognizes Ronnie, and goes to see Ann—angry that she has not saved herself for *him*—he calls her honesty (her not lying to him or to Ronnie) "filthy." Upset and furious, she shows him the door. The next day, Bogard goes out on the torpedo boat, and Claude is blinded. Claude tells Ann to marry Bogard and live a normal life; as a blind man, he says, he has no use for a wife. They have always been honest with each other about their not being in love, and Claude forces her not to start lying about it now. But when he insists that he *wants* her to go, Ann clutches him and says, "No! You're lying! Now you're lying!" (As is typical in Faulkner's screenplays—and novels—the scene ends on this note of maximum tension.)

Ronnie learns that Bogard is to be assigned a virtual suicide mission: to bomb a heavily guarded cruiser that will otherwise interfere with a vital offensive. Bogard accepts the job, and there are several good scenes of the variously brave and cowardly reactions of his crew. When he hears the news, Claude insists that he and Ronnie torpedo the cruiser instead. They leave a note, passing the "care" of Ann on to Bogard. Bogard tries to stop them, but arrives too late; he and McGinnis fly to the battle site anyway. The torpedo mechanism jams, and Claude and Ronnie decide to ram the cruiser with their boat, torpedo and all. Just before they crash, Claude catches up with Ronnie in their game of "Beaver."

At this point Faulkner cuts, as he had in his original story, to the military dispatches that describe the climactic battle, and Bogard's going on to bomb the ammunition depot and enemy headquarters. (In the margin of the screenplay, Hawks wrote that the battle ought to be shown rather than described.) The screenplay ends with Bogard and Ann, now married—as she had prophesied in childhood—placing a memorial to Ronnie and Claude in the chapel of the town where they grew up. Bogard is angry with himself for not dying when they did (shades of *Sartoris*), but Ann insists that he did all he could. Faulkner retains the ending of his story, however, while still managing to work Ann into it:

> BOGARD: Yes. God, God. If they had only all been there: generals, the admirals, the presidents, and the kings—theirs, ours, all of them!
>
> ANN: Hush. [Draws his head down to her breast, holding it there] Hush—hush.

Hawks was again pleased with the script, but a problem arose. The children who were to play Ronnie, Ann, and Claude for the first quarter of the picture turned out to be unable to master British accents. Faulkner was in Mississippi, proofreading *Light in August.* Accordingly, Hawks turned over the script to two professionals, Edith Fitzgerald and Dwight Taylor, instructing them to lengthen the battle scenes and write out the children. The screenwriters apparently found that without the childhood scenes the adolescent scenes made little sense, and decided to abandon the entire first half of the story. By this time the picture was entitled *Today We Live*, which roughly translates: "Now that the war is over, and Ronnie and Claude are dead, Bogard and Ann can marry." (Fortunately, the picture is better than its title.) At Hawks's summons, Faulkner returned to Hollywood to make some revisions in this final screenplay, adding one scene that the reader will by now recognize. Just before Claude goes out on the run that will blind him, Ann tells Ronnie of her love for Bogard. Ronnie assures her that Claude will get over it.

> ANN: I didn't want you to say that. I wanted you to understand.
> RONNIE: I do.
> ANN: Then don't ask me to let Claude down, not when things are like they are.
> RONNIE: Stout fellow!
> ANN: That's what I wanted you to say. Say it again.

At this point Ronnie kisses her, for the first time in their lives.

Today We Live opens with Bogard (Gary Cooper) arriving in England. The Boyce-Smiths' father has just died in combat, and Ann (now Diana; Joan Crawford) has put the family mansion up for rent. Claude (Robert Young) and Ronnie (Franchot Tone) are about to be posted for

France; Ann and Claude decide to marry when the war is over. After the soldiers have left, however, Ann and Bogard fall in love. (The suddenness of their declarations is not believable.) Bogard enlists; Ann goes to France as a nurse. From this point, things go on more or less as described above, with Bogard becoming an aviator, running into Claude, and so on. The dialogue, however, is as clipped as it was in the story—much more so than in Faulkner's screenplay—and the picture got bad reviews on that account. The battle scenes are among Hawks's very best, and Oliver T. Marsh's cinematography is as sharp and moody as that of Karl Freund or Gregg Toland. The picture is rarely seen today and deserves a revival.

Back at MGM, Faulkner began an extremely ambitious screenplay. His assignment was to adapt John McGavock Grider's novel *Diary of the Unknown Aviator*, on which various MGM writers had been working since 1926 under the titles *War Birds* and *Honor*.[5] He had turned in a treatment some time before, dealing with the wartime exploits of John and Bayard Sartoris. In December 1932, MGM okayed the grafting of this treatment onto *War Birds*, and Faulkner found himself with the opportunity to revise and expand *Sartoris* for the movies.

Sartoris is the chronicle of a family rather like Faulkner's own. From generation to generation the sons bear the names John (after John Sartoris, a railroad magnate shot down in the street by a political opponent) or Bayard (after Bayard Sartoris, an impetuous soldier who was killed in the Civil War by a Northern cook from whom he was trying to steal a tin of anchovies). The oldest living Bayard, as the novel opens, is—like Faulkner's grandfather—a banker; the climactic event in his life (described in a much later collection, *The Unvanquished*) was his decision to face but not shoot the man who killed John, his father. In spite of old Bayard's repudiation of violence, the names John and Bayard bear into the next generations the "Sartoris" code of impetuosity, honor, pride, and violent death. Most of the novel concerns old Bayard's relationship with his grandson (hereafter, Bayard), who returns from the First World War in the grip of a self-destructive depression. Bayard's twin brother, John, had been shot down by a German pilot despite Bayard's attempts to keep him from going up in an unsafe plane; John had even shot at Bayard for trying to stop him. Bayard's anger at himself for surviving John, and the oppressive sense of death and emptiness with which the war has left him, drive him to three desperate acts: he buys a fast car and eventually crashes it, indirectly causing old Bayard's death; he marries Narcissa Benbow (from *Sanctuary*) and abandons her, pregnant; and he tests a plane that comes apart in mid-air (*cf.* Roger's death in *Pylon*). When Narcissa's child is born, she refuses to name him John, in the hope that the curse will vanish with the name. The novel leaves one with the impression, however, that this is an inadequate exorcism; it was not until his 1938 story "An Odor of Verbena" (the final chapter of *The Unvanquished*) that Faulkner deliberated at length on the solution to the family's—and the culture's—troubles in old Bayard's refusal to gun down his father's killer. Not until 1938, that is, if one makes the mistake of excluding the screenplays from Faulkner's oeuvre.

John and Bayard's wartime experience continued to interest him. *Sartoris* was written in 1928–29; in 1931 he published two stories about the brothers. "Ad Astra" tells how Bayard encountered a captured German pilot—an aristocrat on the run from his heritage—in a bar shortly after the Armistice. "All the Dead Pilots"—which Faulkner for a long time considered his finest story—tells of John's fight with his captain (Spoomer) over the affections of a French girl. Whenever Spoomer is going to visit the girl, he confines John to base; John retaliates by releasing Spoomer's dog, who either invades the food supplies or tracks Spoomer to his rendezvous. The two men finally have it out in the girl's bedroom: Spoomer hides, John steals his clothes, and Spoomer is forced to return to base dressed as a woman. Spoomer is disgraced, and John is transferred to a Camel squadron for punishment; flying his Camel too gloriously, he is shot down.

These additions, evidently, did not satisfy Faulkner; in 1932–33 he dramatized in *War Birds* not only the "whole" of the brothers' conflict over John's behavior, but also the gist of the family's moral liberation. Unlike *Turn About*, which is written almost like a play (at one point Faulkner even describes an action as "offstage"), *War Birds* is broken up into shots and has fully-detailed camera movements. If it is not Faulkner's finest screenplay (that laurel goes, I think, to *Dreadful Hollow*), it is certainly one of his best.

War Birds opens in the early 1930s. In spite of his fate in *Sartoris*, Bayard here has not gotten himself killed. He lives in Jefferson with John's wife (Caroline) and son (Johnny); also in residence are a German (Luther Dorn) and a Frenchwoman (Antoinette). In the first scenes, Johnny figures out that Dorn is the man who shot down his father, and that Antoinette was his father's mistress. Johnny goes to his mother and demands to be told the whole truth; Caroline reads him John Sartoris's wartime diary (which is how Faulkner works in the *Diary of the Unknown Aviator*). In flashback, then, the story unfolds, with the pages of the diary functioning as a visual icon for John's narrating mind.

The first half of the flashback[6] is closely based on "All the Dead Pilots." Antoinette is the object of John's quarrel with Spoomer. Bayard disapproves of John's promiscuity (he is married, after all), and John resents Bayard's big-brothering. The scene in which Spoomer sneaks back as a peasant woman is played for laughs, rather than simply alluded to (as it is in the story); instead of being put out of commission, however, Spoomer is left in command. He uses his power to get his enemy transferred to the Camel squadron, and John becomes obsessed with trying to shoot down Spoomer, just as Bayard spends much of his time trying to stop him from doing so. Antoinette gives up her loose ways and devotes herself (although he rejects her) to John's care—doing his laundry in secret and praying for him. During an air battle John zeroes in on Spoomer's plane, and Bayard forces him down, shooting in his direction and flying over him. The next time this situation arises, John fires a burst at Bayard (the same action as in the novel, but now more clearly motivated); a German plane, bearing the insignia of a skull smoking a pipe, finishes John. Bayard lands, searches out Spoomer, and fires at him point-blank with a pistol that is inconveniently empty. He then begins to search for the flyer who killed his brother; knowing there are only a few hours till Armistice, he finds the skull-marked plane and shoots it down.

At this point Faulkner brings in "Ad Astra." During a celebration of war's end, Bayard discovers that the German pilot (Dorn) has survived and been captured. Dorn tells his story, a fight breaks out, and Dorn saves Bayard from a well-aimed bayonet. Bayard takes Dorn to his room, where Antoinette is waiting. Dorn disarms Bayard, then returns the gun after relieving Bayard of his obligation to him (for saving him from the bayonet) by reminding Bayard vividly of the way John died. Bayard considers for a moment, then decides not to remain the killing-machine the war has made of him. He throws the pistol through the window, where it leaves a star-shaped hole. The image fades out; the "star" brightens.

The part of the story that follows John's death has been "told" directly by Caroline; she goes on to tell Johnny how Bayard decided to bring Dorn and Antoinette home with him, because in them—and their memories of John—his brother survives. (This ethic is emphasized at the end of *The Wild Palms*, where Harry decides not to kill himself because it is only in his memory of Charlotte that their love endures; "between grief and nothing," he says, "I will take grief.") Johnny goes out to confront Dorn and Antoinette, and forgives them. Dorn refuses to excuse what he did; he insists only that war is never "fair." The three of them turn as Bayard jumps the gate on horseback; they salute him. As he slows his horse and returns the salute, the image dissolves, and the film ends as "in dissolve there passes behind Bayard the ghost of John's ship, John looking down at them, his face bright, peaceful. The ship goes on in dissolve; sound of an engine dies away."

John's ship has been seen before: it accompanied Bayard as he searched for the German plane. Here it functions, like the brightening star, as a symbol of acceptance, reconciliation, and survival. It is in *War Birds*, then, and not in *The Unvanquished, The Wild Palms*, or *Requiem for a Nun* that Faulkner discovered the way out of the "waste land," that place where the dead confront their furious, ghostly impotence until it destroys them. The point of "Ad Astra" and "All the Dead Pilots" had been that the war had left its survivors empty and lost (like the blind Claude in *Turn About*, with "no use for a wife"). Faulkner's switch here might be dismissed as a Hollywood happy ending, did it not so eloquently anticipate the ethics of his later fiction. In this screenplay, much more successfully than in *A Fable*, Faulkner shows how it is possible for wars to *end*, and with them the compulsions that doom and obsess so many of his characters.

At one point in *War Birds* Faulkner calls for a "kaleidoscopic double exposure," the Hollywood stepchild of montage; it is worth noting that he does not yet know the term. In his next screenplay, referred to as *Mythical Latin-American Kingdom Story*, Faulkner uses montage not only for the conventional purpose of indicating the passage of time, but also to alternate two *kinds* of printed message. The story concerns Otto Birdsong, a drunken airplane mechanic (like Jiggs in *Pylon*) who has deserted his wife and daughter early in the war. Mrs. Birdsong's appeals in the Personals column of the paper (which exhaust her limited funds) are intercut with the headlines that describe the progress of the War and the Depression. The sequence ends:

[7] HOOVER ORDERS TROOPS TO DISPERSE BONUS MOB OF UNEMPLOYED.
[8] Otto. Where are you? I am sick. M.
[9] NATIONS AGREE DISARMAMENT WILL BE CURE FOR WORLD BANKRUPTCY.
[10] JAPANESE TROOPS ENTER GREAT WALL.
[11] You don't need to hide anymore. She died last night.

These cuts are bridged by dissolves, but the montage aesthetic, however simplified, is clearly at work. *Latin-American Kingdom* has some interesting and no doubt coincidental connections with Hemingway's later novel, *For Whom the Bell Tolls*—notably a hard-headed revolutionary named Maria Rojas. It was dismissed by the script department as "a very ordinary story, with one or two characters that might have been very interesting if the author had taken the trouble to develop them."

From there it was downhill as far as MGM was concerned. After his lackadaisical behavior on the set of *Lazy River*, his contract was allowed to lapse. He was called back to Hollywood by Hawks, who wanted him to adapt *Sutter's Gold* (a project first tackled by Eisenstein). That film never got past the treatment stage—although it may well have influenced Faulkner's plans for *Absalom, Absalom!*, since both are stories of drifters who "strike it rich" and whose love-lives reflect their ambitions. By December 1935 Hawks had persuaded 20th Century-Fox to hire Faulkner as co-screenwriter on *The Road to Glory* —then called *Wooden Crosses*, after a French film which the studio had bought for its battle footage.

Between his stints at MGM and Fox, Faulkner had been at work on *Absalom, Absalom!*, one of his greatest novels. He had bogged down in it, and had asked Hawks for advice. His friend suggested that Faulkner write about something besides "those damned hillbillies"; Faulkner came back at him with a story he knew about a couple of flyers and the woman they share, and Hawks said, "Well, write that." *Pylon* relieved some of the pressure built up by *Absalom, Absalom!*, but within eight months of its publication Faulkner suffered a severe loss: his brother, Dean, was killed in a plane accident. When he came to

Fox, then, he was brooding about Dean's death as well as actively trying to finish the passionate, brilliant, draining *Absalom, Absalom!* He warned Hawks that he was not likely to do his best work; Hawks warned him not to get drunk till the picture was finished. In this emotional maelstrom Faulkner completed what he referred to as "the best novel yet written by an American" (tossing the only copy onto the desk of a fellow screenwriter), began his love affair with Meta Doherty Carpenter, and collaborated on one of Hawks's finest films, *The Road to Glory*.

Wooden Crosses (1932) was no ordinary film about trench warfare; all of the actors were French veterans, come together after fourteen years with the intention of showing what the war was really like. It had its premiere at the Geneva Disarmament Conference, and was so powerful that (as French critic Georges Sadoul reports) one veteran tried to kill himself after seeing it on television in 1962. It tells the story of Gilbert Demachy, a sensitive intellectual who joins a squad of the 39th Infantry in 1915, all but one of whom die in the course of the picture. As the *New York Times* Paris correspondent described it, the film ends with Demachy's "dying alone in the slime of a deserted battlefield, while over his head in a symbolic procession file an array of the dead, each carrying his wooden cross."[7]

All five of the preliminary screenplays for *The Road to Glory* end with a variant of this ghostly procession, and feature a pianist and student turned soldier (Lieutenant Michel Denet). The release version dispenses with the ghosts, but retains most of the battle scenes. It *has* a metaphysic, however; rather than emphasize this parade of the dead, *The Road to Glory* dramatizes a cyclical view of history whose repetitions generate a sense of timelessness. Men die, but the regiment continues; neither the beginning of the war nor its end is in sight, or relevant. In a structure that remarkably anticipates religious philosopher Mircea Eliade's study, *The Myth of the Eternal Return*,[8] this film shows how it feels to live in a timeless state, where history is continually erasing itself and returning to its point of origin. The regiment's leader (Captain Paul LaRoche), for instance, gives the following speech to his men each time they go up to the front:

> Soldiers of France, you are now members of the Fifth Company, Second Batallion of the 39th Regiment of the Line. This regiment was created by General Bonaparte and served gloriously with him through many campaigns. It also served in the Crimea, in Indo-China and in Africa. Since 1914, it's been fighting on this front. Its record of valor has not yet been damaged. I do not expect any man or any platoon or even an entire company to add stature to that record, but I do and will require that no man in it detract from that record.

LaRoche keeps himself going with doses of aspirin and cognac. At the end of the film, when he has died and been replaced by Lieutenant Denet, his successor gives the men this identical speech (the third time it has occurred in the film—always with that "*now*"), then returns to his quarters—and LaRoche's former lover—tossing a handful of aspirin into his mouth. The regiment continues; some of the men in it are new; each trip to the front is as much the first time as it is one in an infinite series. Within this context, there can be little permanent, historical, recorded achievement; "glory" is a strictly existential value.

Perhaps, as the following scene indicates, one is now at the heart of what Faulkner means by "say it again." Early in the film, LaRoche (Warner Baxter) is in his quarters with his lover, the nurse Monique (June Lang). She is apprehensive about his safety; he gives her a rosary and says, "This was given to me by—by someone I love very much—my sister." She accepts it, says she will pray for him, and then thanks him for his *kindness* to her.

LAROCHE: Is that all?

MONIQUE: Oh Paul, it—it tears my heart each time you go back to the front.

LAROCHE: Wait a minute. Do you know what you just said? Say it again.

MONIQUE: It tears my heart.

LAROCHE: Goodby.

MONIQUE: Goodby.

LAROCHE: I'll come back—I always come back. I'm eternal.[9]

When he does come back, one is tempted to argue, he does so as Denet (Fredric March). This "eternal return" transcends the personal, and throws an entirely new light on the individual's relation to history—a problem with which Faulkner was just then struggling in *Absalom, Absalom!* In the draft of *Wooden Crosses* he wrote with Joel Sayre, Faulkner not only called for the treble repetition of the commander's speech, but even had Denet make his appearance as a mock corpse, rising from a flower-stuffed hearse at the start of the picture.

One of the talents Hawks most valued in Faulkner was his ability to reinvent scenes Hawks had used in previous films, repeating them in a way that made them new. In this case he wanted to re-use the triangle from *Today We*

Live: two men love the same girl, and the man with the earlier "claim" sacrifices himself when he is blinded in battle. Hawks was also re-using the title of his first film (*The Road to Glory*, 1926) and a basic plot-line from his 1930 film, *The Dawn Patrol*, in which one officer (here Denet) criticizes the commander of a squadron with a high death rate (here LaRoche), until he himself inherits the command. In keeping with its own metaphysic, *The Road to Glory* repeats all these structures without seeming repetitious.

After the rosary scene, Monique leaves and Denet reports for duty. Although Denet is a good soldier, he is also something of a flip intellectual, and he criticizes LaRoche's "rations" (aspirin and cognac) as well as his record: half of the company dies on each trip to the front. As Sergeant Regnier (Victor Kilian, more recently seen as *Mary Hartman*'s Grandpa Larkin) explains, the men refer to themselves as "Captain LaRoche's hard bargains." LaRoche makes his speech, and the men move up, after LaRoche rejects an elderly volunteer as unfit for service. After several exchanges in which Denet plays hero (trying to save a soldier caught on a wire) and LaRoche is established as a hard-headed but not insensitive leader (shooting the wire-caught soldier after Denet has failed to rescue him and lost another man in the process), the men discover that the Germans are digging *under* their quarters and setting mines. When steel helmets are issued, the film's principal comedian, Bouffiou (Gregory Ratoff), sits on his. The company outlasts the diggers, but looks back at the point of relief to see the platoon of reinforcements blown to smoke.

In the interim before their next deployment, both LaRoche and Denet have love scenes with Monique (Denet has met her earlier, during an air raid). When Denet realizes that Monique is LaRoche's lover, he calls off the affair, but LaRoche discovers the rosary in Denet's room. The next time they go up, another old man demands the chance to serve; he turns out to be LaRoche's father (Lionel Barrymore). LaRoche rejects him too, but the old veteran bribes Bouffiou into burning the order of transfer. Under the name Private Morain, Papa LaRoche moves up with the company, earning his place there by throwing himself on what turns out to be a dud grenade. "Morain" carries the bugle he blew at "the last charge at Sedan," and talks so much about his lack of fear that the audience realizes he is something of a coward. When Denet, Regnier, Bouffiou, and the old man go out on a wiring party, "Morain" panics and throws a grenade at what he thinks are Germans, killing Bouffiou in the process. Regnier, who is dying of a bullet wound, asks Denet to tell LaRoche that he (Regnier) threw the grenade, but when Denet tries to do so, "Morain" confesses and is put under arrest by his son.

Back at the hospital where he is recovering from an arm wound, Denet finds Monique and confesses his inability to stop loving her; she feels the same. They embrace, then turn to find LaRoche staring at them. They plead for his understanding, then discover that he has been blinded by a head wound. LaRoche forgives Monique, orders Denet to assume command, and then appoints himself as Communications Detail: he will direct an artillery barrage from the telephone outpost established by the wiring party. Since that outpost is directly in line with the target, this assignment is suicidal. To redeem himself, "Morain" says he will be his son's eyes on the mission (a perfect Barrymore line). Just before the fatal shell hits, LaRoche allows his father to blow the ancient bugle. In the closing scene, Denet gives his men the speech and swallows the aspirin, indicating that he has taken on the strain *and* the ethics of command. (John Ford "steals" this for the ending of *Fort Apache*, by the way, where John Wayne dons a cap with Henry Fonda's sunshade.) Although he and Monique are now together, there is no suggestion that they or their love will survive the war; it is still only "1916, Somewhere in France." The final image is not a parade of the dead, but a shot of the exploded bugle—itself an icon of "survival" and repetition.

One final note about *The Road to Glory*. For all their similarity to the male couples in Hawks's films, Denet and LaRoche are also recognizably Faulknerian. In the first draft especially, Denet is an artist and a heavy drinker. LaRoche is described by Monique (not unsympathetically) as "twisted inside—but he's not dead inside." The scenes between LaRoche and his father are extremely affectionate and moving, but the key to LaRoche's character is his great love for his sister—a love he attempts to transfer to Monique. His realization of *that* failure is one aspect of his suicide, and in that respect he is similar to Quentin Compson—who in *Absalom, Absalom!* is described as already half-ghost, caught in some timeless place between history and annihilation. Although much of the film's dialogue was written by its associate producer, Nunnally Johnson, and the device of the rosary is indebted to Zanuck's "suggestion" that there be some prop that could link Monique and Denet, it is clear that the shooting script was assembled (out of its many drafts) by Hawks and Faulkner, and that the film as released is primarily their work.

Most discussions of Hawks compare him at some point

with his friend John Ford. Faulkner's career at Fox suggests another point of contrast between these masters: where Hawks tried to use every script Faulkner wrote for him, Ford consistently rejected (or was not assigned) those written for *him*. Ford's *Drums along the Mohawk*, *Submarine Patrol*, and *Four Men and a Prayer* are almost entirely free of Faulkner's contributions. The writer/producer with whom Faulkner regularly worked at Fox, Nunnally Johnson, liked him personally but felt he had little talent for screenwriting, and wrote Faulkner's windy dialogue and complex motivational structures almost completely *out* of both *Slave Ship* and *Banjo on My Knee* before shooting on each began.[10] It was 1942 before any of Faulkner's work again reached the screen, and again the director was Hawks; the studio, however, was Warner Brothers, and the working conditions can only be described as oppressive. Faulkner was put on script after script to which Warner's had no serious production commitment and in which Faulkner had little or no personal interest; they were trial screenplays, requiring only a small corporate investment (Faulkner's subscale salary) but a great deal of the *time* Faulkner felt he should have been spending on his fiction.

The two scenes he wrote for *Air Force* reveal his continuing commitment to doing good work for Hawks. In the first, a corporal from Brooklyn vents one of Faulkner's favorite gripes about California: "The sun shines and nothing ever happens, and before you know it you're sixty years old." The second scene occurs two-thirds of the way through the film: the dying Captain Quincannon (John Ridgely), surrounded by his crew in a base hospital, imagines that he is "taking off" into the sunrise. The original death scene (by Dudley Nichols) was sentimental in

Museum of Modern Art/Film Stills Archive   Courtesy of MGM

TODAY WE LIVE (1933)

Ronnie (Franchot Tone), Diana (Joan Crawford), and Claude (Robert Young) admire their catch: a gladiatorial cockroach named Wellington.

Museum of Modern Art/Film Stills Archive Courtesy of 20th Century-Fox

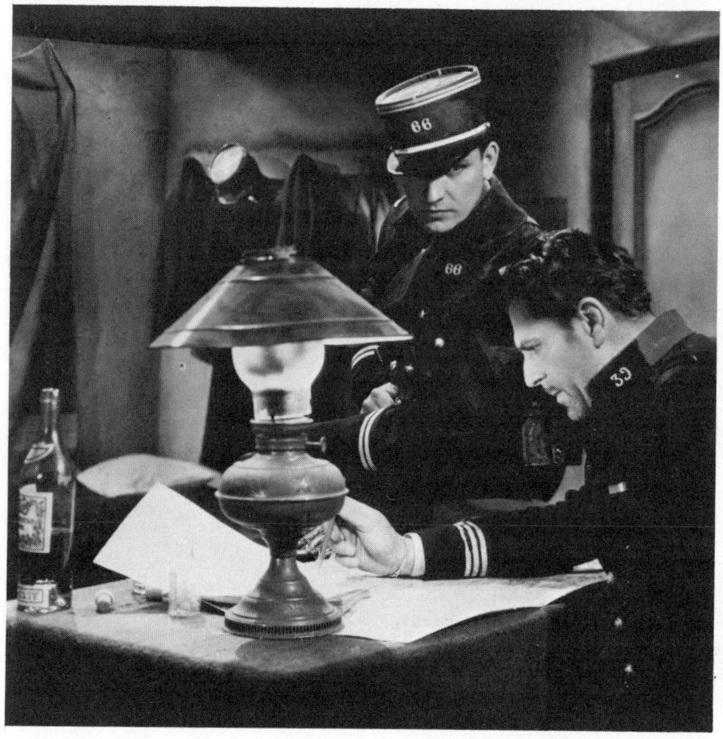

THE ROAD TO GLORY (1936)

Lieutenant Denet (Fredric March) and Captain LaRoche (Warner Baxter) confer on troop deployment. LaRoche's bottles of aspirin and cognac figure prominently here—emblems of the strain of command.

Museum of Modern Art/Film Stills Archive   Courtesy of Warner Brothers

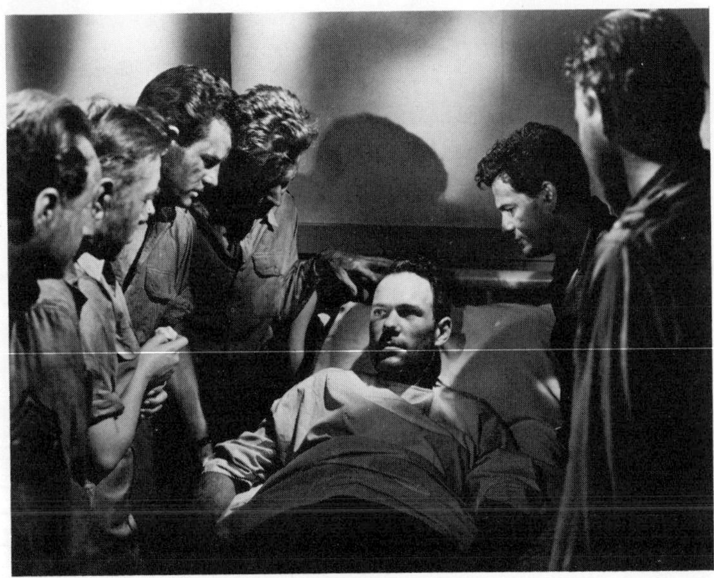

AIR FORCE (1943)

The dying Captain Quincannon (John Ridgely) prepares for "take-off," surrounded by the crew of the *Mary-Ann.*

Museum of Modern Art/Film Stills Archive Courtesy of Warner Brothers

TO HAVE AND HAVE NOT (1944)

Marie (Lauren Bacall) interrupts Frenchie (Marcel Dalio) and Harry Morgan (Humphrey Bogart). The composition indicates the relative importance, in Morgan's mind, of politics and sex.

Museum of Modern Art/Film Stills Archive Courtesy of United Artists

THE SOUTHERNER (1945)

Grandma (Beulah Bondi), Sam Tucker (Zachary Scott), Nona Tucker (Betty Field), and their malnourished children give thanks for a meal of possum. In a few seconds, Grandma will reach for the first and biggest helping. Since there are no vegetables or milk to be had, this meal will not stave off the daughter's pellagra. Like many of Faulkner's blacks and poor whites, the Tuckers will "endure"; in this scene, the elements of faith and failure are equally prominent.

Museum of Modern Art/Film Stills Archive Courtesy of Warner Brothers

THE BIG SLEEP (1946)

Marlowe (Humphrey Bogart) picks himself up after being worked over by Eddie Mars's toughs, while Jones (Elisha Cook, Jr.) watches.

TO HAVE AND HAVE NOT (1944)

Howard Hawks, Humphrey Bogart, and Lauren Bacall between takes on the set.

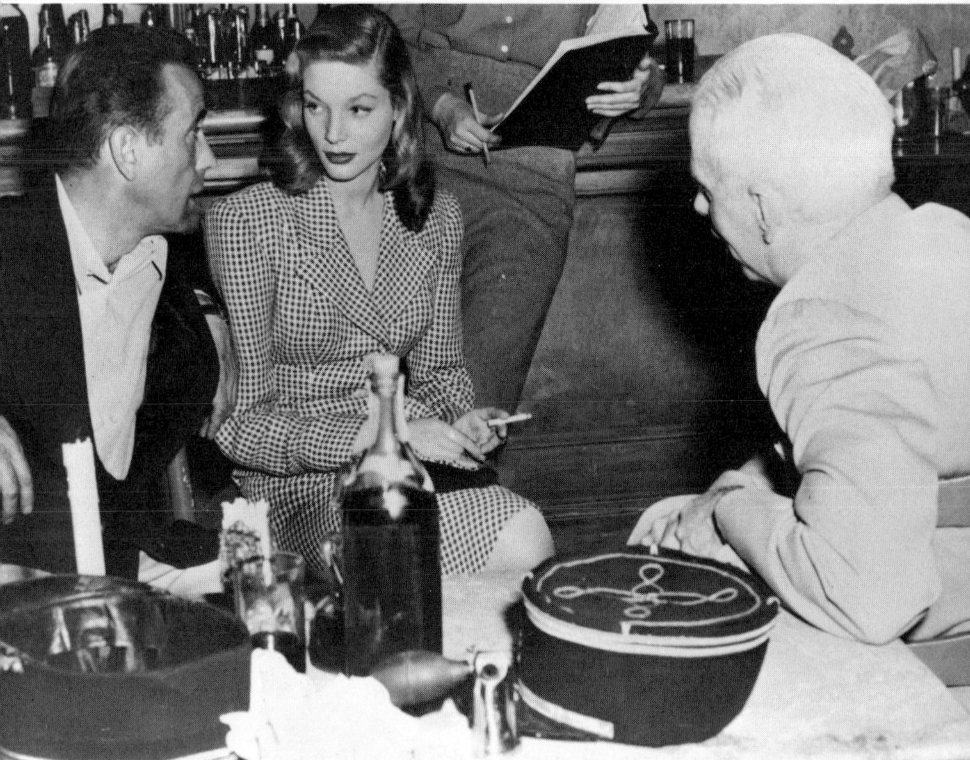

Museum of Modern Art/Film Stills Archive   Courtesy of 20th Century-Fox

THE SOUND AND THE FURY (1959)

Jason (Yul Brynner) reveals the concern and care that underlie his attempts to control Quentin II (Joanne Woodward).

Museum of Modern Art/Film Stills Archive Courtesy of 20th Century-Fox

SANCTUARY (1961)

Temple Drake (Lee Remick) in a "low down" moment with Candyman (Yves Montand), just before one of his associates sends Candyman off on a disastrous liquor run.

THE REIVERS (1969)

Boon (Steve McQueen) briefs Lucius (Mitch Vogel) and Ned (Rupert Crosse), just outside Miss Reba's brothel in Memphis.

Museum of Modern Art/Film Stills Archive
Courtesy of Cinema Center/National General

Courtesy of Paul Roebling

TOMORROW (1971)

Jackson Fentry (Robert Duvall) in a rare moment of happiness, riding with his father and adopted son in a truckful of cotton.

Courtesy of Paul Roebling

TOMORROW (1971)

Sarah (Olga Bellin) meditates on her fate, soon after Fentry finds her outside the sawmill.

the extreme; what Faulkner achieved was both moving and professional, emphasizing not the death of one man but the solidarity he inspires in his crew. Hawks's organizing device for this film—the impact of the war on the men of the bomber *Mary-Ann*—stimulated Faulkner to construct his own vision of the war around the history of a single plane. *The Life and Death of a Bomber* follows its plane from factory to combat, and emphasizes the conflict between the self-sacrificing attitude taken by American workers and soldiers, and the undermining of their efforts by greedy corporate management. The bomber, constructed improperly to save money, becomes the symbol of a value-system that must be reexamined if America is to succeed in not only a military but also a cultural sense. This treatment was, of course, not approved for expansion or production.

In 1943 Faulkner put in serious work on three properties that were never produced. The first, *Country Lawyer*, is a study of racial, generational, and class conflict in Jefferson, Mississippi; it is the complement of *Go Down, Moses*, which Faulkner had published the year before.[11] The second, *Battle Cry*, was to have been Hawks's epic military film, one that might have borne the relation to his other war pictures that *Red River* bears to his westerns; it was abandoned at the final screenplay stage when Warner's refused to approve Hawks's multimillion-dollar budget. One of the sequences Faulkner wrote for this film suggests that the wartime solidarity of blacks and whites —dramatized in the relationship between "America," a black soldier whose wound "immobilizes him and causes him terrible agony, although he gives no outward sign of being in pain," and Akers, a white Southerner who looks after him—will lead to the fulfillment of Lincoln's dream.

The third treatment, *Who?*, was an expansion of an idea suggested by Henry Hathaway and William Bacher: that the "unknown soldier" was Christ reincarnate. Eleven years later, Faulkner published *A Fable*, a novel whose allegorical structure originated as much in the ambitions of *Battle Cry* as it did in the story of *Who?*

One of the things that amused Hawks was the way his friends Hemingway and Faulkner were always asking him about each other, admiring each other's work but refusing to meet. On a fishing trip with Hemingway, Hawks tried to interest him in adapting one of his own novels for the screen. When Hemingway answered that he was happy as he was, and had no interest in "bucking hours," Hawks called him "a damned fool," then offered this challenge: "I can make a picture out of your worst book." "What," asked Hemingway testily, "is my worst book?" "That goddamned piece of junk called *To Have and Have Not*." "You can't make a picture out of that," said Hemingway, and Hawks replied: "OK, I'll get Faulkner to do it. He can write better than you can anyway."

To Have and Have Not, by the way, is no piece of junk; it is, however, about losers, and as Hawks says, "I *hate* losers." It is the story of Harry Morgan, a tough and bitter fisherman who runs liquor and revolutionaries between Cuba and Florida when his other means of support are exhausted. In the course of the novel he loses his arm, his boat, his shipmate, and finally his life, having learned that "No matter how a man alone ain't got no bloody fucking chance." Harry's wife, Marie, is autonomous, hard, and passionate, but even she is beaten down at the end. In one sense, they both go from having to not having; in another, however, Marie and Harry are the "haves" in this story; the moral "have nots" are the artists and businessmen who loll in their boats and bars, congratulating themselves on their talents.

"You've drawn the character of Harry Morgan," said Hawks; "I think I can give you the wife. All we have to do is make a picture about how they met." For ten days the fishermen drew up that story, switching the location to Vichy-controlled Martinique. Faulkner, as it happened, had recently written *The DeGaulle Story*, an anti-Vichy screenplay, and was quite interested in that aspect of the new picture. With his brilliant collaborator, Jules Furthman, Faulkner expanded the story-outline Hawks had delivered him, turning Morgan into Hawks's idea of a "winner" and Marie into "Slim" (the nickname of Hawks's wife). By the time the picture was finished, however, these characters could hardly be described as anything but Bogart and Bacall.

According to Hawks, Furthman got along well with Faulkner. They had apparently met at MGM in 1933, in connection with *Honor*. Furthman was disliked by many of his collaborators because he was demanding and obnoxious, and also because he owned some of the most valuable real estate in Culver City. He had been forced to move from his former home (to what was then worthless property) because his retarded son's bellowing disturbed the neighbors. It is not far-fetched to speculate that Furthman warmed up to Faulkner as the creator of Benjy. Hawks enjoyed working with Furthman because he could taunt him into doing good work. When Furthman wrote a scene for *To Have and Have Not* in which Marie has her purse stolen, Hawks teased him until he stalked out and wrote the scene in which Marie steals a wallet. (Hawks was quite as direct with Faulkner, but less loud.)

To Have and Have Not is central to Hawks's work, but

marginal to Faulkner's. It might even be considered marginal to Furthman's, since most of the script was thrown away on the set. A great many extraliterary elements influenced the picture: for one, Warner's was interested in making another *Casablanca*, and wanted emphasis thrown on Bogart's conversion from isolationism to Resistance activity; for another, Bogart did not want to have to deliver the kind of lengthy patriotic speech Faulkner had been writing for Warner's for the past two years. Furthman had become expert at creating tough female roles—he worked on several pictures for Josef von Sternberg and Marlene Dietrich—but the character of Marie, for all her resemblance to other Furthman heroines, is largely the result of Hawks's and Bacall's improvisations, with some help from a chorus girl Hawks calls "Stuttering Sam," who had been around quite a bit herself. The *Casablanca* influence extended beyond Jack Warner's directives; Hawks had once swapped assignments with the director of that film, Michael Curtiz (who had been stumped by his assignment, *Sergeant York*), and was now going to show, rather playfully, how *he* might have made *Casablanca*. Faulkner's work is most evident in the characterization of the Resistance fighters (particularly the woman), and in the treatment of the themes of patriotism and fear. The film's basic device was hit on by Hawks during that first fishing trip: each of the losses suffered by Hemingway's Morgan (notably those of his money and fishing tackle) pushes Hawks's Morgan deeper into an involvement not with politics but with politicos, some of whom he likes and therefore helps, some of whom he dislikes and therefore fights. Where considerations of expediency lead Hemingway's Morgan to consider killing his rummy shipmate, Eddie (played in the film by Walter Brennan), Hawks's

Morgan continues to support his old friend because Eddie used to be a good man and has stuck by him. An unspoken law in Hemingway's novels is that a man with a healthy emotional life will at some point in the story be castrated or killed or otherwise sexually ruined; Hawks reverses this structure completely, leaving Morgan not dead and bankrupt but autonomous, witty, politically engaged, and sexually fulfilled. Faulkner probably did not find these changes distasteful; the point is that he did not make them.

The next piece of work on which Faulkner was seriously engaged was *Fog over London,* a projected remake of an Edward G. Robinson/Humphrey Bogart vehicle, *The Amazing Dr. Clitterhouse.* Clitterhouse is a psychiatrist whose interest in the criminal mind leads him to become a criminal himself, to observe his own reactions. A headline in one of the newspapers describing the doctor's trial reads, "Jekyll or Hyde?" Faulkner apparently took his cue from this line, and from Victor Fleming's recent version of *Dr. Jekyll and Mr. Hyde* (starring Spencer Tracy), whose major departure from the earlier films made from Stevenson's story was to emphasize Jekyll's pleasure in being Hyde, and Jekyll's theories about the need to accept and understand one's darker self. Faulkner used a number of visual devices to indicate that Clitterhouse has genuine criminal impulses beyond his control; the split that develops between his good and bad selves eventually leads him to suicide. The original *Clitterhouse* had ended with a comical murder trial whose verdict the doctor himself had called "amazing." *Fog over London* met the same fate as the earlier *Banjo on My Knee,* and for the same reason: Faulkner was going too deeply into the motives and troubles of his characters to suit the producers.

The superstars of *To Have and Have Not* were reunited on *The Big Sleep*, Jules Furthman excepted. Contrary to legend, Furthman had nothing to do with the screenplay as published; he was called in only when shooting was nearly completed.[12] His assignment was to condense the final third of the screenplay into a few brisk scenes. For one thing, the film was getting too long; for another, the censors had refused to pass the ending devised by Faulkner's collaborator, Leigh Brackett. Hawks challenged the censors to give him a better ending, and to his surprise they outlined the extremely crisp and violent scene that now closes the picture. That scene was written by Furthman and Hawks, long after Faulkner and Brackett had gone on to other projects.

The Big Sleep went through three major stages of generation, and it will simplify this discussion to clarify them at the start. The first temporary screenplay was written by Faulkner and Brackett in eight days; Faulkner outlined the story and divided up the work. They expanded this into a final screenplay,[13] which was rejected by the censors. Furthman wrote most of the new final scene, then helped Hawks condense the rest during shooting. Warner's liked the picture so much that they decided to hold up its release for more than a year, so that it finally came out as part of Warner's "twentieth anniversary of sound on screen." During the interim, however, it was shown to American servicemen overseas; their reactions led Hawks to write and shoot several new scenes, most of them romantic banter between Philip Marlowe (Bogart) and Vivian Sternwood (Bacall). When the picture was released, then, it was much faster and funnier than Brackett and Faulkner had intended. Hawks began with a "film noir," a hard-boiled detective story with sexy undertones;

he ended with a wacky, elliptical, contradictory film that, because it plays by no known rules, decisively influenced such New Wave films as Godard's *Breathless*, Truffaut's *Shoot the Piano Player*, and Chabrol's *A Double tour* (*Web of Passion*), not to mention Altman and Brackett's later version of Raymond Chandler's *The Long Goodbye*. As Hawks told a group of critics before its release, "You're not going to know what to make out of this damned picture; it holds out its hand for a right-turn signal, then takes a left."

Chandler's novel is romantic, fog-bound, and depressing. It is set in an expanding, poisonous Los Angeles, paving itself into an ethical oblivion. Its hero-detective, Marlowe, is more than tough: he is a throwback to the old virtues of professionalism, honor, and integrity. On the novel's first page Marlowe describes a stained-glass panel in the Sternwood mansion, "showing a knight in dark armor rescuing a lady who was tied to a tree and didn't have any clothes on." This panel is a miniature of the entire novel, in the course of which this knight in unshining armor learns that "knights had no meaning" in the Sternwoods' chess game.

Marlowe is hired by General Sternwood to protect his nymphomaniac daughter, Carmen, from a blackmailer. What really upsets the General is the possibility that the villain is Rusty Regan, the husband of his other daughter, Vivian. Several murders and reversals later, it develops that Regan was killed by Carmen when he rejected her advances, and that Vivian is collaborating with a gambler named Eddie Mars, protecting Carmen and misleading Marlowe. The climax occurs when Carmen tries to shoot Marlowe (who in his turn has rejected her), near the sump in which Regan's body has been mouldering. Vivian sends Carmen to a sanitarium, the General is kept in the dark, and Marlowe feels that he has been made "a part of the nastiness now." Such an ending, of course, could not possibly satisfy Hawks, and a variation of the cleanup he had called for in *To Have and Have Not* soon came into play.

Faulkner and Brackett, working on alternate sections of the script, downplayed Chandler's imagery of existentially empty eyes, cyanide factories, oil wells, and a fog so thick that one of the characters is described as leaning against it, leaving the question of visual atmosphere to Hawks. They reduced the number of scenes in which Marlowe and various policemen explain who killed whom and why, but left in enough to make it *possible* to follow the story. Neither they nor Hawks, however, could figure out who killed the Sternwoods' chauffeur; Hawks wired Chandler, who didn't know either, so the matter was left unresolved.[14] The major change they introduced was to make Marlowe and Vivian Sternwood fall in love and plan to marry. This necessitated two related changes: Regan became the General's employee instead of Vivian's husband, and Vivian became not tough and evil but strong and good/bad. Carmen (Martha Vickers) remained the villain, but Brackett introduced (and Chandler approved) a marvelous climax, set not at the sump but in the house of the now-dead blackmailer, Arthur Geiger. Marlowe enters the house, outside which Mars (John Ridgely) and his gunmen are waiting to shoot him when he leaves. Carmen arrives; she had been locked in her room, but climbed down a drainpipe to rendezvous with Marlowe, whom she intends to seduce. (This part of the scene is Faulkner's contribution, an echo of Quentin II's escape in *The Sound and the Fury*, as described—and misremembered—in the

1945 Appendix to that novel.) When Marlowe rejects her, she shoots at him with a gun he has unloaded; then she taunts Marlowe who, because of his love for the General (Charles Waldren), could never reveal the truth about her and cause a scandal that would break the old man's heart, if not kill him.[15] Marlowe snaps off the light as she leaves the house, so that Mars—thinking he is shooting Marlowe—guns her down. Mars enters, and Marlowe kills him. Marlowe tells the General that Carmen has died in a car crash, and that Regan "sends you his affection and respect, but he won't come back." The General, Marlowe, and Vivian come to a happy end, and Carmen and Mars are punished—but the censors would not stand for Marlowe's causing Carmen's death.

As the picture now ends, Marlowe and Vivian are at Geiger's with Eddie Mars; Marlowe forces Mars to go out and be shot by his own men, then arranges with Vivian to have Carmen "sent away" to be cured. It is in this final scene that the series of crimes is "explained," much too fast for the audience to put it together. Even if one could follow this speech, however, one would find that it contradicts most of what has gone before, making Mars out to be the principal villain. This is more of a fast curve than the plot can support; it is at this moment, then, that *The Big Sleep* blasts the genre of detection and teaches the audience how to "read" film in a new way. One follows the action because it is action; one responds to each scene on its own terms, without probing beneath them for some secret, coherent structure. The first half of the film, then, which is played much as Faulkner and Brackett wrote it (except for Hawks's interjection that Marlowe and Regan are old friends—which allows Marlowe to take a personal and masculine interest in the case—and a number of comic scenes), gives the audience the impression that all the clues will form *some* kind of pattern. Furthman, however, cut out almost all of the later explanatory scenes and introduced (as the censors had demanded) the nearly impossible suggestions that Mars had been deluding Vivian and that Carmen might not have killed Regan. Hawks compounded this shift by adding romantic scenes that completely derail the rhythm of Marlowe's quest and the audience's attempt at concentration, and by directing the picture for *speed.*

The genesis of one crucial scene shows the interplay of these creative forces and gives a sense of how Faulkner saw the story. In Chapter 24 of the novel, Marlowe enters his apartment and finds Carmen, naked, in his bed. Her "small sharp teeth" glint; her giggle reminds him of "rats behind a wainscoting in an old house." There is a chessboard on his card table, with a problem he can't solve; he moves the knight, then tells Carmen to get out. Then he moves back the chess-piece: "Knights had no meaning in this game. It wasn't a game for knights." Carmen curses him; her eyes are blank, and her lips move "as if they were artificial lips and had to be manipulated with springs." He realizes that he cannot endure her violation of his home, the only private space he has. When he threatens to throw her out by force, she gets dressed and leaves. The imprint of her body on the pillow and sheets drives him into a fury, and he tears the bed to pieces "savagely."

In Faulkner's version of this scene (#123), Carmen and Marlowe have a long exchange of cute, witty dialogue; Carmen (in the chair, dressed) is still bent on seduction, but also meditates on her fall from what she thinks is innocence. As in the novel, she has a nervous habit of biting her thumb; she appears to be doing this throughout the scene, but when Marlowe tells her to take her thumb and get out, she shows him that she is biting the white queen from his chess set. The scene continues:

> Marlowe stares at her for a moment, then he slaps her terrifically across the face, rocking her back. The chessman falls from her hand and she stares at Marlowe, frightened now, as he walks toward her.
>
> CARMEN: Do that again.
> MARLOWE: (seething with repressed rage; almost whispering) Get out.
> CARMEN: Maybe if people had done that to me more often, I would have been good now.
>
> Marlowe reaches her, grasps her arm, hurries her across to the door, jerks the door open, almost hurls her through it, flings the wrap after her, slams the door, turns the bolt as she rattles the knob, then begins to hammer on the door. He turns and crosses the room rapidly to the bath while she still beats on the door, and washes his hand savagely with soap and water, his face now actually beaded with sweat. . . . [He then pours Scotch on his hand, "when what he needs is carbolic acid."] . . . While the knocking still continues, he kneels at the hearth, lays the delicate chess-piece on it and with a heavy fire-dog hammers the chess-piece into dust, still beating even after the piece has vanished, his blows at last drowning out the sound of the knocking on the door.
>
> FADE OUT.[16]

Allowing for the censors, this is the finest adaptation of Chandler's scene one could hope for. Marlowe's thoughts are expressed in action, and both chapter and master-scene black out on an image of Marlowe's "savage" attempt to destroy the effects of Carmen's intrusion on his privacy and all that it represents. It is the one place, in novel and screenplay, that he *cracks*—where one sees that the Sternwoods have left their mark on him. Faulkner introduces a significant change in emphasis, however, evident in the shift from knight to white (virginal) queen. The issue now is not male honor but female dishonor, not the threat to his professional code but the violation of his image of womanhood. Although this change of chess-piece can be explained as a means of compensating for the necessary writing-out of the bed and its nude defiler, it is a change that is typical of Faulkner's moral imagination. (It was less than one year after finishing *The Big Sleep* that he wrote the Appendix to Malcolm Cowley's *Portable Faulkner*, in which he portrayed Caddy Compson as the mistress of a Nazi official; in a lighter version of the same tone, he identified her husband of 1920–25 as "a minor moving picture magnate.") Faulkner's Carmen surpasses all her sources—in both Faulkner and Chandler—in her capacity for innately sexual evil.

When Hawks rewrote this scene, he kept Faulkner's humor but dropped any indications of strain on Marlowe's part. Both chess-piece and -game are dispensed with; instead, Carmen starts to bite her thumb (which irritates Marlowe), thinks better of it, and then says, "See, I remembered." When Marlowe advises her that he has a tough friend, she asks, "Is he as cute as you are?" and he answers, "Nobody is." While we can all be grateful for this wonderful line, the climax of the scene is disappointing. Marlowe simply throws Carmen out after she bites his hand. She tries to protest; he says "Shut up" and slams the door; then there is a quick fade-out. There is no breakdown, no still point, no resonance. When I told Hawks that I thought he had wrecked the scene, he told me I didn't understand the picture. After thinking about it for some time, I realized he was right.

The point is that Hawks had no intention of putting Bogart through the kind of professional crisis and moral self-examination basic to a picture like *The Maltese Falcon* and to Chandler's novel. *The Big Sleep*, on its surface, is dark and violent *fun*. The undercurrents of perversity and amorality succeed in disturbing the audience because they are so rapidly and efficiently passed over. Hawks's Marlowe, like his Harry Morgan, is a winner who can take his licks. When the darkness does surface, it is in connection with other characters—notably Jones (Elisha Cook, Jr.) and Canino (Bob Steele), whose deaths are the strongest moments in the picture. Yet even these brilliantly violent scenes are counter-balanced by the comic interludes Hawks improvised on the set, such as Bogart's impersonation of a prissy book-collector and his subsequent encounter with Dorothy Malone (by far the sexiest bookseller on film). The next time Faulkner handed Hawks an evil, lusty woman—Princess Nellifer in *Land of the Pharaohs*—Hawks had no idea how to balance her out, and the picture flopped. Although there is no place in Hawks's universe for Faulknerian depravity, it is unfortunate that the two men could not have worked out some compromise on the character of Vivian, who is simply too *good*-under-it-all to hold up her end of the story. It is possible, of course, that the problem with Vivian is Bacall, who is visibly being coached by Bogart in most of her scenes, and who (thanks to Jack Warner) has the burden of being Vivian and Slim at once; it is, in any case, her least effective performance.

In 1944–45, then, Faulkner went through a highly successful period of screenwriting, a creative spurt comparable only to that of his first year at MGM. The three pictures that reached the screen—*To Have and Have Not, The Big Sleep*, and *The Southerner*—are classics, and even if Faulkner did not write the complete shooting scripts for any of them, the experience of seeing at least *some* of his work produced was gratifying, and perhaps led in itself to his working so hard, and with such optimism, on *Fog over London* and *Stallion Road*, both of which are good scripts, and both of which were not used.

Jean Renoir, the director of *Grand Illusion* and *Rules of the Game*, had been working in the United States since 1941, most often with Dudley Nichols (of *The Informer, Stagecoach, Air Force, For Whom the Bell Tolls*) as screenwriter. The script for *The Southerner* was written by Renoir and Nunnally Johnson, then revised by Faulkner (whose exact contributions remain to be established). It may be that Renoir, who was familiar with Faulkner's fiction, chose him to polish dialogue and write a few scenes after realizing the Faulknerian quality of his story; it is just as possible that Faulkner took their story and changed it to one of his own. Whatever the case, *The Southerner* distinctly echoes *The Hamlet* and *Go Down, Moses* in both ethos and setting.

Sam Tucker (Zachary Scott), his wife Nona (Betty Field), his maddening irascible Grandma (Beulah Bondi), and his children try to make a go at tenant-farming rather than to work on salary for a conglomerate. Sam's goal is not money but autonomy; when his friend Tim (Charles Kemper, the narrator of the film) urges him to work in a factory rather than starve, Sam says he would rather grow beans than live in the city where all people grow is dollars. So although the Tuckers arrive at their new shack deployed (visually) among their belongings almost exactly as are the Snopeses in "Barn Burning," the values they represent are the opposite of Snopesism. Sam has two major antagonists: the weather—which ruins his cotton crop at the end of the picture—and his neighbor, Henry Devers (J. Carroll Naish). Devers is an Ab Snopes figure and even has some of Ab's lines from *The Hamlet*; he is not a climber like Flem, but a tense and selfish farmer who begrudges the Tuckers' use of his well and sends his pigs to ruin their vegetable garden when it looks as if they are going to succeed with their farming. When Sam's child contracts pellagra and the doctor prescribes milk and vegetables, Devers (who has the only cow) makes Sam watch as he dumps gallons of milk into a pig-trough. Devers has two goals in life: to buy up the land Sam is farming when Sam fails, and to catch Lead-pencil, a huge catfish. Things are resolved between the men when Sam discovers Lead-pencil on his own line (an echo of Faulkner's story, "Hand upon the Waters," in which a drowned body is found snagged on a trotline) but agrees to let Devers take credit for the catch. Sam's problem with the weather cannot be so easily resolved; the only thing to do is endure. One is faced with the same sort of paradox that arises when discussing Hawks and Faulkner: the parts of *The Southerner* that most directly echo Renoir's other pictures—in this case the Tuckers' battle with despair, the contrast between city and country, and the complex ways nature is presented—can also be described as Faulknerian. Faulkner considered Renoir the best contemporary director;[17] as with Hawks, this respect made it possible for Faulkner not just to write good scenes but to collaborate on a level so intimate it defies analysis.

The final work of this period, *Stallion Road,* is an adaptation of Stephen Longstreet's novel about a veterinarian's struggle to perfect an anthrax serum, and the love that develops between him and Fleece Tucker, a horse-rancher. The vet, Larry Hanrahan, has a tough and honest relationship with his assistant, Pelon, and a hostile and bitter one with Daisy Otis, a young married woman who would kill him sooner than see him marry Fleece. Faulkner's screenplay, which was rejected by Warner's for no defensible reason, tells a complex and satisfying story with remarkable economy. It is an entirely professional job—*not* "New Wave," as Longstreet has described it,[18] but still compelling, witty, linear, and well-paced. Visually, it is similar to *Turn About.* The dialogue resembles that of *The Big Sleep*: funny, biting, occasionally vicious, fast. The themes he emphasizes are those of hard work (counterbalanced by self-destructiveness), male bonding, honor, class-conflict, the evils of lust, and the virtues of intelligent strength. There is no point in suggesting that this screenplay be produced—it is a creature of the 1940s—but it certainly ought to be published.

In the early 1950s Faulkner wrote two last scripts for Hawks. His screenplay for *The Left Hand of God*—by all accounts decisively superior to that used in the Dmytryk film—was shelved on the advice of a priest, who told Hawks that the picture would turn Catholic audiences against him. *Land of the Pharaohs* was filmed as written, but is of only thematic interest. Faulkner described the story as another *Red River*, with the Pharaoh (Jack Hawkins) amassing treasure and constructing his tomb in the same spirit as John Wayne had built up his cattle herd and driven it to market. It is just as easy, however, to note the similarities between *Land of the Pharaohs* and *Ab-*

salom, Absalom!: Pharaoh's plans for the great pyramid obsess him precisely as Sutpen's "design" does him, and in both cases the overreachers are destroyed by their compulsions. The evil princess (Joan Collins), as suggested above, arose more from Faulkner's nightmare of "abomination and bitchery" (*Light in August*) than from Hawks's views of women. As in *Absolution* the hero gives up everything "for a woman who was not worth it." Even the lifelong friendship between Pharaoh and the priest Hamar (Alexis Minotis, the narrator of the film—as was Walter Brennan in *Red River*), which is directly comparable to the male/male relationships in so many of Hawks's films, is introduced by a scene that could have come from *Turn About*:

> PHARAOH: You know I can't resist gold.
>
> HAMAR: Yes, I know. The first fight we had as children, remember, we fought for a little gold ring that had been a gift to me. You won the fight and took the ring.
>
> PHARAOH: You tricked me into some wager and got it back before nightfall—remember that?
>
> HAMAR: And you have been fighting for gold ever since.
>
> PHARAOH: And mean to keep it forever.[19]

Pharaoh's central compulsion, which originates in a childhood fight, determines the entire tragedy. The theme of blindness recurs too, although this time the blind man is an artist whose son serves as his eyes (a reversal of the end of *The Road to Glory*). Although Hawks mainly remembers the fun he and Faulkner had in devising a system of sand hydraulics to seal the pyramid, it is clear that the two men were engaged as well in an intimate thematic collaboration. In *Land of the Pharaohs* their points of imaginative contact are strikingly obvious, and the film rewards study if only for that reason.

It is worth pondering, in conclusion, what might have happened if Faulkner had teamed up with someone besides Hawks in 1932. D. W. Griffith—whose *Intolerance* is constructed like *The Wild Palms* and whose *The Birth of a Nation* had impressed Faulkner as a child—was in Hollywood at the time, out of work. Eisenstein had just finished his work in Mexico, and was desperate for projects. MGM had some business connections with Abel Gance. There is no telling what kind of scripts he might have written for these men, nor any way to gauge their potential impact on film history. As it was, Faulkner learned his craft from a man who distrusted "fancy cutting," refused to use flashbacks, and believed that the director's job was to "tell a good story." He learned that craft well and worked hard at it. Although he almost never used the cinematic techniques of his fiction in his films, he managed whenever possible to write about the characters and themes that mattered to him as a novelist. In this fashion, his two careers were integrated throughout most of his creative life, and the myth that he wrote films resentfully, sloppily, and mercenarily deserves to be laid to rest.

5 REVOLT IN THE EARTH AND DREADFUL HOLLOW

In order to assess Faulkner's strengths and weaknesses as a screenwriter, and to discover whatever connections he might have perceived between the aesthetics of film and of fiction, I would now like to examine two of his screenplays in depth. The first, *Revolt in the Earth*, is a loose adaptation of the montage novel, *Absalom, Absalom!* The second, *Dreadful Hollow*, is an original horror film. Neither of these has yet been discussed in print—the first, no doubt, because it is so bad, and the second because no one besides Hawks and myself has seen it. Taken together, these scripts resolve many of the paradoxes of Faulkner's two careers.

By all rights, *Revolt in the Earth* ought to have been a

masterpiece. Faulkner's collaborator, Dudley Murphy, was an experimental filmmaker with distinct interests in montage (he photographed Fernand Léger's *Ballet Mécanique* in 1924), in Jungian archetype (he directed the film of O'Neill's *Emperor Jones* in 1933), and in race conflict—all of which are basic to *Absalom.* So for once Faulkner was in a position to collaborate with a filmmaker who might have been receptive to the montage aesthetic of his fiction, and one must wonder at their decision not even to attempt to adapt *Absalom's* techniques for the screen. Even though *Revolt* is not the average linear script, and includes some interesting experiments with superimposition, visual symbolism, and subjective sound, it is in no way comparable to *Absalom*—not in technique, not in thematic integrity, and hardly even in plot.

In 1934 Faulkner had published the story "Wash," in which he described the relationship between Colonel Thomas Sutpen and the white-trash squatter on his plantation who becomes (after Sutpen is ruined by the Civil War) his drinking companion and storeclerk. When Sutpen impregnates Wash's granddaughter, Wash assumes he will do right by her; it develops, however, that Sutpen is interested in Milly only if she gives birth to a son (so that his estate and lineage will not perish; Sutpen's son, Henry, had been killed in the war). When she delivers a daughter, Sutpen insults and rejects her; Wash kills Sutpen with a scythe. When a posse arrives, Wash kills Milly and the infant, then rushes at the men with his scythe, forcing them to shoot him.

This story formed the germ of *Absalom, Absalom!*, which was published in 1936. In his novel Faulkner explored the reasons for Sutpen's compulsion to have a son survive him, and established that Sutpen himself was of hillbilly origins, an "innocent" like Wash. Sutpen came down from the mountains like the Biblical David, confronted the power structure (a big house from whose door he is turned away by a black servant), and decided that the only way to negate his shame would be to make himself as powerful as the unseen aristocrat: to found and dominate a "House." This obsession, which he calls his "design," leads him first to the Indies, where he sires Charles Bon. When he discovers that Bon's mother is part black, he rejects both of them and returns to the South, where he lays claim to a hundred square miles of forest and swamp ("Sutpen's Hundred"), builds a mansion, and marries the white and respectable Ellen Coldfield. Ellen bears him a son, Henry, and a daughter, Judith.[1] Complications arise when Bon shows up in New Orleans. befriends Henry, and pays court to Judith—all with the intention of forcing Sutpen to acknowledge him as his son. Since Bon, as the eldest, would be heir (and, as part-black, unrespectable), Sutpen instead places on Henry the burden of sending Bon away. The war intervenes, but all three men survive. Henry, who has very little idea of Bon's parentage, shoots him in order to prevent miscegenation; he then flees, leaving Sutpen with the problem of getting another son. By this time Ellen has died, so Sutpen propositions her sister, Rosa Coldfield. When Rosa realizes that he intends to marry her only if their child is male, she rejects him. Eventually, Milly accepts the (perhaps unstated) terms of Sutpen's offer. As in "Wash," Sutpen's rejection of yet another innocent leads to his death.

The figure of Sutpen continues to obsess Rosa, who in 1909 tells her version of this story to Quentin Compson. Quentin, who is in the grips of his loss of Caddy, and who is described as on the verge of becoming a "ghost" himself

—of surrendering to his doom, and to the force of the past—identifies with Henry and seeks out the rest of the story from his own father (who tells it rather differently). Quentin and Rosa go out to Sutpen's Hundred, where Clytie (Sutpen's half-black daughter) has been hiding Henry for years; Henry and Quentin meet, in a scene which is delayed till the novel's final chapter. At Harvard, Quentin tells the story to his roommate, Shreve, after he has received a letter from his father informing him of the deaths of Rosa, Clytie, and Henry. Quentin and Shreve then spend a long night filling in the gaps in the story, each spurred on by an identification with both Bon and Henry, and by some power in Sutpen's story that compels itself to be told and uses the boys as its mediums. By the end of the night, Quentin is a mass of ambivalence, and his forthcoming suicide has been much more dynamically motivated than it ever was in *The Sound and the Fury*.

The basic device in *Absalom* is that of a voice turned against itself: Quentin arguing with ghost-Quentin, Quentin telling and inventing with Shreve, Quentin and Shreve dialectically engaging the power of the self-telling story, and so on. The novel is characterized by an agonized, compulsive rhetoric, and projects the tension of absolute unresolution. In every sentence, Faulkner tries to reflect, restate, and intensify the dialectic of all these forces—"to say it all in one sentence, between one Cap and one period."[2] Although there is not the sudden cutting between past and present that characterizes *The Sound and the Fury*, there is an omnipresent sense of conflict-through-juxtaposition; it is appropriate, then, to call this a montage novel, even if the rhetoric's intent is to transcend fragmentation. The brilliance of the novel depends, in fact, on Faulkner's awareness that such transcendence is impossible, and his consequent attempt to construct the novel for maximum unresolution. His compulsion to "say it all" resembles Sutpen's obsession with his design, Rosa's with Sutpen, and Quentin's with the story; all of them begin with this undifferentiated compulsive stream, find it breaking into fragments (words and scenes) when they try to express it, surge forward in spite of their awareness of necessary failure, and stop only at the point of exhaustion—at which point the tension renews itself, and they try again.

It *would* be possible to tell this story on film, by cutting between the talkers and what they know or invent, by letting the contradictions accumulate, and by exploiting the inherently dialectical nature of classical montage. It would not, however, have been possible to sell such an idea to Warner Brothers in 1942, and that is really the only excuse *Revolt in the Earth* might have. The crucial point about *Revolt* is that it makes it appear unlikely that Faulkner considered film as serious a medium as fiction. Although he might have been aware of the connections between what he and Eisenstein were doing (as *The Wild Palms* suggests), he evidently felt that there was no point in attempting to tell so complex a story on film: or perhaps he simply did not know how to do it. In any case, *Revolt* depends on a condensation and simplification of *Absalom* that is so radical and so downright inane that it might be better to call it an amplification of "Wash."

Whereas Faulkner described *Absalom* to his publisher as "the story of a man who wanted a son through pride, and got too many of them and they destroyed him," he described it to Nunnally Johnson as simply "about miscegenation."[3] Neither is an adequate description, but the latter indicates what Faulkner considered that aspect of the story which could be sold to Hollywood. *Revolt* is not even particularly about miscegenation; its main concern is with voodoo.

Dudley Murphy's *Emperor Jones* had used drumbeats, chants, and double exposure to dramatize the way Jones is hounded by his past—both by his deeds and by his racial unconscious. It is a fairly powerful film, and the odds are that Murphy's directing could have made the voodoo drums, galloping horsebeats, and demonic laughter that punctuate *Revolt* function effectively. Faulkner had already explored (with Nunnally Johnson in *Slave Ship*) the organizing device of the curse: the slave ship begins in blood and must end in blood, as a convenient "old man" prophesies—in person, at the start of that screenplay, and voice-over, at its conclusion. *Revolt*'s entire text, it should be noted, is consistent in style and typography with the rest of Faulkner's Hollywood writings; it is likely that Murphy and Faulkner discussed the project together, but that Faulkner did all the writing.

Revolt has a fairly promising beginning: a fade-in on a marble statue of Colonel Sutpen, banked by "formal yet lush shrubbery. In the background a broad sweep of grounds and colonial mansion. As CAMERA BEGINS TO RETREAT, the sound of a galloping horse begins. The CAMERA PICKS UP Clytie, a child of twelve, a mulatto, who is watching the statue with a grave, rapt, still gaze. Accompanying the hooves, the wraith of a horse and rider crosses the scene between Clytie and the statue. It is gone, but the sound of the galloping hooves continues on through [a] DISSOLVE INTO: INTERIOR OF A NEGRO CABIN."[4] (This is similar to Faulkner's description of Wash's meditation on Sutpen: ". . . thinking went slowly and terrifically, fumbling, involved somehow with a sound of galloping hooves, until there broke suddenly free in mid-gallop the fine proud figure of the man on the fine proud stallion . . ."[5]) In the cabin, Clytie has just been born. She is apparently not Sutpen's child, but the devil's, as an old black woman intones.[6] Sutpen, who has stopped in to pay his respects, discounts the idea that "my family is under the displeasure of nigger witch doctors one jump from Africa, eh?" but the old woman's curse is apparently a reflection of the truth: "When de devil spawns on Sutpen land dey'll be a revolt in earth till Sutpen land has swallowed Sutpen birth." What is apparently satanic here is miscegenation; as soon as Sutpen fails to destroy the child, the curse takes hold.

The next scene (which may be in Clytie's memory, or simply a flashback) shows Sutpen's pleasure at the birth of a calf, and his subsequent rejection of Milly's child. Wash attacks Sutpen with a jug, but is beaten back; Wash's whole family, then, survives this encounter, and Wash's great-granddaughter goes on in her turn to have a son, also named Wash.

It is soon established that Sutpen has two legitimate children, Henry and Judith, and that Judith is being courted by Bon (who is no kin to Sutpen). When Henry discovers that Bon has a mulatto mistress and child (as in the novel), he kills Bon so that Judith cannot marry him. Soon afterwards, both Henry and Sutpen are killed in the war. Throughout most of this, a tom-tom has been beating on the soundtrack; now it blends with the drumming of shellfire. The scene of Sutpen's death (with Henry in his arms) dissolves to a voodoo ceremony. Faulkner then cuts to the Sutpen house, which is being overtaken by "jungle," and to the servants' discussion of the "drums in de earth." Upstairs, Judith walks "frantically back and forth to the rhythm of the drums . . . finding each time that she is walking in the rhythm, discovering this with increasing horror each time she breaks her stride." Eventually she runs out to a battlefield, takes a pistol from a dead soldier, and fires at a Yankee officer who "symbolizes the murderer of her father." She misses, and (believe it or not) they marry:

> He grasps her, takes the weapon away from her, and holds her. Judith is hysterical. We hear the drums again, and she looks over her shoulder as if she feared they were behind her.
>
> JUDITH: Take me away!
>
> She is in the officer's arms; this pose is electrified into a photograph of the same people in wedding dress. The laughter carries over the—
>
> DISSOLVE TO:
>
> CLYTIE
> —again standing looking up at the statue. It has begun to be overgrown and stained. The laughter begins to die away. A musical theme enters. It is martial, and perhaps we hear the bugle call to cease firing which denotes the end of the war. A black man approaches, and the music has in it something of sadness and fortitude. The man tries to attract Clytie's attention, but she doesn't respond. Tom-toms grow out of the music as she continues to watch the statue. . . . Then suddenly Clytie turns with a rhythmic movement almost in time to the music and she and the negro embrace.
>
> DISSOLVE TO:

SOUND OF TOM-TOMS CONTINUES
Out of fading dissolve come the separate birth cries of three children.

The children are born to Milly's daughter, to Clytie, and to Judith. Judith hears tom-toms in the delivery room, and the doctor insists that her Yankee husband take her to Europe. He does so, and Judith becomes a great lady. Clytie gets letters and photos from her, and watches as her own grandson taunts Milly's grandson (Wash) with his disinheritance. Wash, staring at the houseboat where the first Wash lived (a shack, in *Absalom*), becomes obsessed with the notion of carrying out the curse. (He is, of course, a Sutpen too.) Wash grows into a version of Conrad's Mr. Kurtz and makes himself the head of a voodoo cult. He sends his evil influence across the Atlantic and lures the only other surviving Sutpen—Judith's granddaughter, Miriam—back to the old plantation, to her doom.

Miriam, who is the cliché heroine-in-distress, has just married Eric, who exceeds all clichés in his irritating stupidity. Eric wants to study voodoo and takes Miriam back to the States. Judith, hearing the news in the middle of the night, falls down a staircase to her death. A great deal of parallel cutting establishes that Wash is responsible for all this; dissolves and more complex optical effects establish that Clytie is telepathic. At this point Faulkner downplays the fact that Clytie is the "devil's scrub" whose birth occasioned the whole problem and shows her attempts to save Miriam from Wash—mainly by threatening him with the bleeding rib of a pig. Eventually Miriam is "swallowed" by quicksand, Wash drowns while attempting to get away from Clytie, and Eric loses *some* of his obtuseness. Now that there are no more Sutpens, a snake slides away from the Colonel's statue, and the screenplay ends.

Aside from the fact that *Revolt* does no justice to *Absalom*, it is also an extremely poor horror film. One could make up an interesting analysis of it as "Faulkner's *Heart of Darkness*" or as a "drama of the conflict between the white and half-white Sutpens" or as a "Jungian treatment of racial and generational trauma"—but the screenplay will not support it. Even if by some chance Faulkner had all that on his mind (and the Wash/Kurtz connection seems likely), he made a botch of it. There seems little point in delaying Wash's vengeance on Sutpen with such complex apparatus. When Faulkner showed him the screenplay, Robert Buckner of Warner Brothers wrote him a "private and confidential" telegram; he thanked him, but went on: "Quite frankly, Bill, I cannot imagine your having had any share in it. I think it is a very badly conceived story with no possibilities whatever for a motion picture. I hope if you had nothing to do with it that you will not let it get around with your name on it. Please forgive me if I seem too presumptuous about this, but I have so high a regard for you as a writer that I refuse to be disillusioned."[7] It should be emphasized that Buckner is not reacting to the theme of miscegenation, or the failure of the screenplay to live up to *Absalom*, or any kind of box-office pressure, and that he writes from a position of respect. I see no reason to disagree with his judgment here. *Revolt* has some interesting visual effects and is significant as Faulkner's most formally experimental screenplay; nevertheless, the story *is* badly conceived, the dialogue is ludicrous, and the whole effort has more loose ends than the jungle-growth around Sutpen's statue.

It was after writing *Revolt* that Faulkner managed, as he told Malcolm Cowley, to lock his movie work "off into another room." Attempting to break his contract with Warner's late in 1945, he described himself as having done "the best work I knew how on 5 or 6 scripts,"[8] only two of which (*To Have and Have Not* and *The Big Sleep*) were filmed. So even if he had movie work in a separate conceptual space from that in which he labored on his fiction, he was not contemptuous of his Hollywood efforts. It seems likely to me that *Battle Cry, Country Lawyer*, and *Stallion Road* make up the rest of the five serious efforts for Warner's, with *Fog over London* or *The DeGaulle Story* a potential sixth. None of these scripts relies on the montage aesthetic of his fiction; each of them is in some way connected, however, with the themes of that fiction. The difference between the two "rooms" in which Faulkner worked, then, seems to have been formal and structural rather than thematic. Without being patronizing, he managed to express his intellectual and emotional concerns within the genres and syntactic modes of conventional narrative film. A script like *War Birds*, which is both structurally and thematically related to the fiction, can be used to characterize the earlier period of Faulkner's screenwriting, when he did not feel the need to keep the "rooms" entirely separate. *Revolt in the Earth* reflects, if anything, a period of structural *and* thematic crisis: the "rooms" are in some ways merging, in others becoming excessively polarized. With the crisis resolved, however, Faulkner went on to write some of his most conventional, entertaining, *and* interesting screenplays: notably *The Big Sleep* and *Dreadful Hollow*.

Dreadful Hollow, unlike *Revolt*, is a brilliant horror film, and reflects an absolute and apparently effortless mastery of the genre—not only of its devices but also of its mythic resonance. It was written sometime in the late 1940s (my best guess), under direct commission from Hawks. In its time, *Dreadful Hollow* (supervised by someone like Val Lewton, whom it would have suited) could have become one of the period's greatest and most troubling horror films. If it were filmed today (and Hawks has some plans for it) it could be modified to suit the talents of Ingmar Bergman (*Hour of the Wolf*) or Roman Polanski (*The Tenant*), but never—for instance—those of William Friedkin (*The Exorcist*). Compared to *Dreadful Hollow*, a film like *The Exorcist* is both ludicrous and gross. Faulkner's work here is so genuinely frightening and so profoundly humanist that it demands comparison with the best of the genre: with *Vampyr, Nosferatu, Cat People, Isle of the Dead, The Wolf Man, The Black Cat,* and the like. It is, after all, one mark of a great horror film that it projects a system of values whose ability to endure (usually via the comic subplot) is validated only with reference to *its own* tragic complement (the horror-figure). This is the sort of structure Faulkner was born to explore—and had been exploring, in terms of race- and class-conflict, of "doom," of "endurance," of self-destruction, and of the Christian mythos, in such works as *Light in August, Go Down, Moses, Absalom, Absalom!, The Sound and the Fury, Sartoris,* "Ad Astra," and even *A Fable*. In *Dreadful Hollow*, then, he does not so much "transcend" the genre as rise to it.

The heroine of *Dreadful Hollow*, Jillian Dare, arrives in the town of Rotherham Halt (204 miles from London), where she has been engaged as companion to the elderly Countess Czerner. She is given a lift from the train to "the Grange" by a witty doctor/poet named Larry Clyde, who is fond of quoting *Macbeth* and drives a small, beat-up car rather like Faulkner's old Ford. (The hero of *Stallion Road* is also a doctor named Larry, and a drunk; Faulkner seems to have intended to caricature and romanticize himself in both these portraits.) Larry calls Miss Dare "Miss Muffet," a joke that masks his awareness that she is about to sit down next to something worse than a spider. She dislikes the joke and his long-windedness and assures him that she can take care of herself. Larry leaves her at the Grange and continues to what he calls "Little Rotting-off-the-map," where he is the only physician.

Jillian is met at the door by Sari, a grim and strong old peasant who has lived with the Countess since childhood. The only other servant is Jacob Lee, an idiot. When Jillian is introduced to the Countess, she is struck by the way the old woman holds out her claw-like hands toward the fire, as if to draw all its heat into her dying body, and by the odd contrasts in her face: old wizened skin, raven hair, young eyes, and strong teeth. Because she needs her job in order to support her mother and crazy sister, Jillian tries not to become unnerved by the rest of what she observes: the way the Countess eats, for instance—tearing out the red heart of a peach, covering her plate with bones as she feasts, insatiable—or the garlic wreath Sari takes from her own room and hangs above Jillian's door. The next morning she finds Sari draining the blood from a heap of pigeons into a bowl—for a pudding, she explains. When she next encounters Larry, he recites a quatrain from Tennyson's *Maud*:

> I hate the dreadful hollow behind the little wood,
> Its lips in the field above are dabbled with blood-red
> heath,

> The red-ribbed ledges drip with a silent horror of blood,
> And Echo there, whatever is ask'd her, answers "Death."

(This works much better than the curse in *Revolt*, and is—along with Dr. Clyde's journal—Faulkner's substitute for the "Book of Vampire Lore" that the genre demands.) Later on, straightening up the library, she seeks out these lines in a volume of Tennyson, and is sufficiently unnerved to scream when she suddenly sees a wolf in the corner; even stuffed, "the wolf is tremendous, it looks like a nightmare, alive." Larry is sent for by Sari, who is afraid that Jillian will become the Countess's prey (as, it is suggested, Sari's own daughter had been), but Jillian refuses to leave. At about this time, a village boy disappears on the way home from school, and Sari informs Jillian that she has sent for some of the Countess's "own people" to come from the Balkans to care for her.

When Dr. Vostok and his Balkan servant arrive, they appear to have brought with them Vera, the Countess's niece: a young, reckless-looking woman who moves languorously and sings in a wild, foreign tone. Jacob Lee installs a huge beam in the ceiling of the Countess's room. Vostok, who is gaunt and strong, is engaged in some kind of battle of wills with Vera, apparently over the person of Jillian. Larry goes to London in an attempt to force Jillian's family to let her leave her post, but Jillian has warned her mother to ignore him. He goes on to the office he used to share with his father, in search of a portion of the old man's records. At this point the series of indirect revelations begins to intensify in speed and deepen in resonance. By the time Larry forces the police to read his father's journal (and they are in any case not far behind him), and to examine the four snake-like hollow teeth Larry's father has saved from his own encounter with the Czerners, it has become clear to the audience not only that Vera is a vampire, but also that she is the Countess, rejuvenated with the blood of the missing child—whose body Vostok has sewn into the stuffed wolf.

Dr. Clyde's journal records how he encountered Count Czerner in a Transylvanian inn, "a tall, striking figure" with "a dark, arresting face" and an air "of contemptuous pride, the air of a man who has suffered so deeply that he is almost beyond hurt." The Count (who is mortal) engages him to pull four teeth from the mouth of his wife, so that she can die in peace. Dr. Clyde agrees only when he has seen this Countess (also named Vera) drop "with languid grace" from her perch on a beam in the ceiling, where she has been draped in something like bat-wings or a cloak. As they watch, her drugged, aged face begins to turn almost young with a "terrifying, vivid flame." After the operation, the Count shows Dr. Clyde his daughter, Vera, who is playing with her peasant companion, Sari, and whom the Count is watching for "the first signs of—her heritage?"

By the time Larry and the policeman (Gregory) return to the Grange, Vostok has set in motion a complex plan that involves killing Jillian, setting fire to the building, and returning to the Balkans with Vera. His actions depend on one of Faulkner's most cherished notions, which is that the dead live on in those who survive them; in this case, the vampire metaphor is horribly ironic, since Jillian, at the sacrifice of her blood, "shall not die, because Czerners do not die." Vostok is foiled, and a chase ensues, at the height of which Sari kills the Countess. As Sari raises her ax "with grief and despair," the Countess screams, "Ingrate! Murderess!" and Sari replies, "Yes, my lady."

On her own deathbed, Sari explains that Vostok was the son of the groom on the Czerner estate, sent off to medical school by the Count in the hope that—since he was obviously in love with Vera—he would be able to take care of her after the Count's own death. (At this point the echoes of *Wuthering Heights*, with its "Grange" and "two-children figures," fall into place.) Vostok and the Balkan are arrested—partly with the help of Jacob Lee, who thereby touches at last "the world of rational men"—and Larry and Jillian agree to marry.

In this hasty summary I have left out most of the action and atmosphere of the screenplay, simply because *Dreadful Hollow* resists excerpting. A few of Faulkner's touches, however, bear special mention. Anyone who has read enough of Faulkner becomes aware of his passion for repeating names—and with them, their attendant doom and glory—from generation to generation. When Vera, daughter of Vera, observes to Jillian that "there is but one woman's face in our family; we all wear it in our turn," one realizes that Faulkner has found the perfect means to express his metaphysics of repetition and regeneration; it is his "ghosts of the past" motif with a vengeance, since Vera is in touch with a death/youth energy that is not only her mother's and grandmother's but also *her own*. Vera is the decisive incarnation of that "doom" in Faulkner's mythos that allows one to die before his own birth (like Hightower in *Light in August*) or to be his own ancestor and progeny (like Quentin Compson, the lovers in *Country Lawyer*, or even the Christ of *A Fable*).

He is also extremely adept at performing twists on stock

lines and figures. When a local woman observes, for instance, that she doesn't want types like Vostok around, "going against the will of God," Larry soberly replies, "Ay. There's enough grief in this world from the ones who are still alive." Such details as the holes in the vampire fangs, and Sari's attempts to keep the Countess alive by fuels other than the blood of the living, indicate the vividness of his imagination—his determination to push the conventional into some new and precise awareness of its potential. It is one thing to construct a scene around a garlic-wreath, another to have Sari give her own to Jillian; just as it is easy to thrill the audience with a cutaway to a stuffed wolf, and another to prepare us gradually—with a shot of a needle and brown thread in Vostok's lapel, and with references to a smell that comes to pervade the house—for the moment when the wolf falls and bursts open, revealing a bloody shoe. Not content to let "Transylvania" and the violent Balkan servant carry the whole burden of mythic decadence, Faulkner has Larry refer in at least three jokes to the Druid and Roman heritage of Rotherham, and makes the idiot, Jacob Lee, as densely prehistoric as *Absalom*'s Jim Bond (whose howl circles into the woods at the end of that novel). The Countess is a magnetic and terrifying figure, comparable not to Dracula but to Sheridan Le Fanu's seductive, relentless Carmilla; her lifelong relation with Sari is explored in such depth that it comes to seem genuinely tragic. Sari's love is echoed by Vostok's commitment to Vera and the Count's to her mother, but surpasses them both in its quality of "grim despair." It is the more to Faulkner's credit that this tragic love-commitment does not make the comic subplot (Larry and Jillian) seem superficial. Where it strikes one, for instance, as an *abso-*

lute mistake to conclude George Waggner's *The Wolf Man* (1941) with a shot of the girl and the "hero" in an embrace, the lovers in *Dreadful Hollow* earn their place in both the historical and dramatic structures which Faulkner has presented; not because they are conventional but because they are strong, they endure.

It appears, then, that Faulkner had considerable skills as a screenwriter, and was able to work in conventional formats when it suited him. He wrote screenplays much as he wrote stories for magazines, with an awareness of market and audience yet without significantly departing from the themes that concerned him in his major fiction. Often he would discover that the complex is not betrayed by the simple—a lesson that his oft-quoted Shakespeare learned in that work which he did for the stage and which he apparently considered much less significant than his sonnets and long poems. And although Faulkner's "plays" are not the equivalent of Shakespeare's, such a parallel is not easily dismissed.

6 FAULKNER'S PLACE IN FILM HISTORY

> They went on; the last glare of the snow faded and now they entered a scene like something out of an Eisenstein Dante.
>
> —Faulkner, *The Wild Palms*

> For example, we have some leaves; and even if Juliette doesn't have much in common with a Faulkner heroine, our leaves could be made just as dramatic as those of wild palms.
>
> —Jean-Luc Godard, *Two or Three Things I Know about Her*

Hiroshima, mon amour and the film *The Sound and the Fury* were released in the same year, 1959. The former, as scripted by Marguerite Duras and directed by Alain Resnais, has more in common with Faulkner's novel than does the latter. In *his* 1959 film, *Breathless*, Jean-Luc Godard has his heroine (Jean Seberg) carry around *The Wild Palms* and quote from it at crucial moments, yet in several interviews he insists that his film is modeled after *Scarface*—an early film by the man Godard once referred to as "the greatest American artist—I mean Howard Hawks."[1] These observations appear paradoxical, but when run to earth they reveal Faulkner's place in film history—a place which has yet to be established or appreciated, and which might surprise Hawks and even Godard as much as it would unquestionably have surprised Faulkner.

That place depends not on Faulkner's films but on the influence of his fiction. It has already been observed that he used such visual tropes as montage, freeze-frame, superimposition, flashback, and perspective distortion, as well as sound-overlap and sound/image conflict in most of his novels, and that his screenplays are recognizable as *his* not because they are visually experimental but because they echo and extend the thematic concerns and occasional rhetorical excesses of his fiction. It should also be eminently clear that those films which set out to "bring Faulkner to the screen" failed to do so because they rejected both Faulkner's techniques and the "metaphysics of time" that (as Sartre observed in 1939[2]) inspired and justified those techniques. A "place in film history" must depend finally on actual released *films* and not on good intentions or abandoned properties. In this sense Faulkner is important as a contributor to the work of Howard Hawks, and as an influence on the work of Orson Welles, Agnès Varda, Alain Resnais, Alain Robbe-Grillet, Marguerite Duras, Chris Marker, and—perhaps most significantly—Jean-Luc Godard: filmmakers who adapted his techniques instead of his stories.

When Herman J. Mankiewicz wrote the screenplay of *Citizen Kane* (1941), he had both *The Great Gatsby* and *Absalom, Absalom!* on his mind. Both of those novels center on the figure of an "innocent" and destructive overreacher whose greatness is appreciated only indirectly, by a secondary character who spends most of each novel tracking down the hero's "real" motives (Nick in *Gatsby*, Quentin in *Absalom*). It is *Absalom*, however, that is the greater influence: first because Jerry Thompson, the reporter in *Kane*, has no direct contact with the deceased hero (as Quentin had none with Sutpen), and second because in both *Kane* and *Absalom* the structure of revelation is much more involuted than that of *Gatsby*. Rosa's Sutpen differs from Mr. Compson's Sutpen just as Leland's Kane differs from Bernstein's; Thompson's revelations accumulate unchronologically, as do Quentin's, and are presented in the order of their discovery, not of their first happening. The burden of Welles's and Toland's camerawork is, as André Bazin observed, to transcend montage—to embrace a variety of conflicting elements within single shots, as Faulkner himself tried "to say it all in one sentence, between one Cap and one period"; but the overall structures of both film and screenplay depend absolutely ón the montage aesthetic, in which times and meanings are butted against each other with little or no explanatory apparatus. It is worth noting in this context that Mankiewicz and Faulkner were both at MGM in 1933, where they might have met; that Toland and Faulkner did meet on the set of *The Road to Glory*; and that both Welles and Mankiewicz were well-read, and might be expected (even in the absence of other evidence) to have been familiar with *Absalom, Absalom!*, which was published four years before the script of *Kane* was composed. And it is hardly an exaggeration to suggest that *Citizen Kane* became, like *The Big Sleep*, one of the most decisive influences on the next generation's sense of structural, tonal, and thematic possibility in the cinema.

Before he won the Nobel Prize in 1950, Faulkner's work was taken more seriously in France than in any other country; in the United States, he had gone virtually out of print, to the extent that Malcolm Cowley had to cut up his own first editions in order to provide copy for *The Portable Faulkner*. His principal champion in France was Jean-Paul Sartre; others included Albert Camus (who adapted *Requiem for a Nun* and who considered Faulkner "America's greatest writer," largely on the strength of *Sanctuary* and *Pylon*), André Malraux, Marcel Aymé, Claude-Edmonde Magny,[3] and Maurice Coindreau (who performed the first critiques and translations). Faulkner's reputation rose along with that of John Dos Passos (whom Sartre in 1938 called "the greatest writer of our time"), revealing the French intelligentsia's interest not just in America but more specifically in the uses of montage.

The Wild Palms was translated into French in 1953 and received much critical acclaim. Within a year, Agnès Varda "had placed together two separate plots in *La Pointe-Courte*, in an imitation of William Faulkner's novel."[4] The editor of that film—which Georges Sadoul has identified as the first New Wave picture—was Alain Resnais.

Resnais's films have dealt with the themes of time and memory more rigorously and brilliantly than those of any other director. It is not simply that they cut freely among past, present, and fantasy, but that their structural complexity is inseparable from their politics, their romanticism, and their metaphysics. In the work of Resnais, the narrative film at last catches up with Faulkner—as in the work of Godard, it finally goes beyond him. It is a considerable part of Resnais's success—as it was part of Hawks's —that he has made a point of commissioning screenplays from his country's major contemporary novelists, all of whom were, by the 1950s, well-versed in the techniques of *The Sound and the Fury* and *The Wild Palms.* This is not just a question of stringing several plots together, but of clarifying their interrelation through the logic of the *cutting.* When Duras and Resnais cut from the heroine's view of her Japanese lover's twitching finger to her memory of an earlier lover's hand in its death-twitch, *Hiroshima, mon amour* asserts the precise visual syntax and transitional logic of the first three sections of *The Sound and the Fury.* And when Robbe-Grillet wrote the screenplay for Resnais's *Last Year at Marienbad* (1961), he not only called for shock-cutting among various times and places, but also insisted that the film *not* depart from the characters' *subjective* impressions of what was happening. *Marienbad* allows whatever contradictions might arise from this narrative method to accumulate and interact in a time which is "not that of the clocks." Where Resnais, in this case, is taking many of his cues from *Citizen Kane*, Robbe-Grillet is demonstrably taking his directly from Faulkner, whom he considered the crucial link between Proust and Beckett in a tradition that he saw culminating in the "radical subjectivity" of the "New Novel" as well as in a new kind of cinema.[5]

This cinema, of course, is not entirely "new," having antecedents in the work of Eisenstein, Gance, Buñuel, Keaton, and others. The point is that Faulkner's fiction kept the traditions of radical subjectivity, montage, and the "metaphysics of time" alive during the period when the coming of sound had rendered montage unfashionable and the economics of the film industry had militated against "visionary" experimentation. Although it remains to be established whether Faulkner hit on these techniques through the films he might have seen in Paris in

1925–26, or conceived them in strictly literary terms (finding most of them in *Ulysses*), it is clear that he is one of the central figures in the cinema's rediscovery of its own narrative—and *anti*-narrative—potential.

One of the decisive factors in the New Wave filmmakers' "rediscovery" of film was Henri Langlois's marathon screenings, at the Palais de Chaillot, of virtually every movie he could lay his hands on. When the novelist Chris Marker directed his Faulknerian investigation of love, time, and memory, *La Jetée* (1962), he set much of its action in the basement of the Palais de Chaillot—an homage to Langlois, as *La Jetée*'s analysis of the "frozen moment" (the memory, or the shot) and of the romantic consciousness as a kind of time machine is an homage to Faulkner. Where Marker, Varda, and Resnais (who were friends) took much of their inspiration directly from literature, the *Cahiers* groups (Truffaut, Godard, Chabrol, etc.) took theirs primarily from what they saw at Langlois' Cinémathèque. Although he was almost certainly aware of their collaboration, then, Godard praised Hawks and Faulkner for entirely different reasons, perceiving—I think accurately—that the two men, for all their complementarity, were important for extremely different reasons and could almost be said to have been working in different worlds.

What Godard learned from Hawks was the impenetrability of speed and the value of precise, classical, unselfconscious, unpretentious directness. Hawks fits Marianne Moore's definition of the interesting artist; he is a "literalist of the imagination," one who shows us things that are important "not because a / high-sounding interpretation can be put upon them but because they are / useful."[6] In the work of Hawks, Godard discerned "an increasingly precise taste for analysis" and a determination not to reach for grandiose romantic effects—although no one could have been better at creating them—but to fix the "basic laws" of cinema "through a more rigorous knowledge of its limits."[7] This could serve as a good summary of Godard's own career, of course, so long as one notes that Godard is more of a romantic than Hawks, and has more difficulty in focusing his classicism. In many of his films Godard has found it necessary to polarize romantic excess and cinematic analysis (in *Pierrot le fou*, for example), to engage them against each other rather than sublimate one to the other.

In his most romantic moments Godard is as likely to refer to Faulkner as he is to a Minnelli musical, since what he first saw in Faulkner was his emotional intensity—what Faulkner himself might have called an indomitable hopelessness. It is likely that Godard returned to Faulkner more than he did to Poe, for instance, because he recognized in Faulkner the difficulty he himself was having in focusing his various loves within a structure that continually skirted incoherence. So that what Godard at last learned from Faulkner was comparable to what he learned from Eisenstein: the value of unresolution. Hawks's world is resolved.

The Wild Palms alternates chapters of two novellas, "The Wild Palms" and "Old Man." In "The Wild Palms" Harry Wilbourne and Charlotte Rittenmeyer run away (with the consent of Charlotte's husband) to live on the outskirts of society. They run out of money and food, and finally out of freedom. When Harry performs an abortion on Charlotte, she dies of an infection; Harry is sent to jail, where he decides to live rather than to kill himself, since his death would obliterate his memory of Charlotte and their love ("*Yes*, he thought, *between grief and nothing I will take grief*"). In "Old Man" a convict is freed long enough to help the victims of a disastrous flood, helps a woman deliver a child, then spends the rest of the story trying to get back into prison, where he feels more safe. This architecture of parallels and contrasts is a classic use of dialectical—in this case, more precisely, *parallel*—montage, but when Godard first refers to *The Wild Palms*, in *Breathless*, he appears to have in mind only the title novella and not the entire work. Instead, he lets *Breathless* itself contrast with "The Wild Palms."

When Patrice (Jean Seberg) meets with a journalist, he gives her a copy of Faulkner's novel, which he calls "a sad story." Patrice is pregnant by a petty gangster, Michel Poiccard (Jean-Paul Belmondo), at the time she reads the book. When Michel suggests that she run off with him, she decides instead to turn him in to the police—who kill him. Toward the middle of this film—whose plot clearly parallels that of "The Wild Palms," and is just as clearly at pains to render those correspondences as ironic as possible —Patrice asks Michel whether he has ever heard of William Faulkner. "No," he says, "someone you slept with?" "Of course not." "Then to hell with him." Patrice reads him Harry's "grief and nothing" line, and Michel responds, "I'd take nothing. . . . Grief's only a compromise, and you've got to have all or nothing." As it develops, then, Michel gets "nothing" and Patrice is left with the burden of remembering him, of trying to understand him, and of having caused his death; she is, in other words, Harry with a difference, and Charlotte as a coward.

In *Pierrot le fou* Godard does let his lovers (Belmondo and Anna Karina) run away with each other but has the woman desert the man, who then paints his face blue and blows off his head with dynamite. The blue paint is one indication, among many, that Godard is still using a stylized and ambivalent self-consciousness to undercut his romantic excesses. In *Alphaville* and *Made in U.S.A.* he turns to both Faulkner and Hawks, having the heroes of both films read—or reincarnate—*The Big Sleep* at crucial moments. But where *Alphaville* sets its detective hero against a Fascistic, computerized Paris-of-the-future (in what is also, fairly clearly, a reflection of the influence of William Burroughs), *Made in U.S.A.* sets its detective-heroine against the more "relevant" and "impenetrable" assassinations of John Kennedy and of Ben-Barka, an Algerian intelligence agent kidnapped and murdered by officials of the French government in 1965. By the time he shot *Made in U.S.A.*, then, Godard was interested more in openly analyzing social and cinematic codes than in alluding to them, and in this enlightenedly Structuralist frame of mind, he again turned to Faulkner.

Made in U.S.A. (1966) was shot, edited, and released at the same time as the film I consider Godard's masterpiece, *2 or 3 Things I Know about Her.* Where the former refers to *The Big Sleep,* the latter refers to "The Wild Palms." Taken together, however, the two films *are* Godard's adaptation of *The Wild Palms.*[8] There is no room here to go into an analysis of the ways the two films reinforce and contradict each other on the way to that "zero point" they both reach, from which Godard felt it was possible to construct a new and politically viable cinema, but it is worth noting that Godard wanted at one point to exhibit the films together, alternating a reel of *Made in U.S.A.* with a reel of *2 or 3 Things,* precisely in the manner of *The Wild Palms.* These films are an extreme example of how to adapt "the spirit and essence" of a work (Wald's phrase) rather than its "story." In fact, Godard has been putting Faulkner on film throughout his career, and it is significant that at the moment when he finally rejects bourgeois cinema—in favor of one that lets the selfconscious audience perform most of the integration and analysis—he is using Faulkner's own central technique of dynamic unresolution.

If it is Faulkner's fiction, then, that has secured his place in film history, what is one to conclude about Faulkner's fate and the fate of his work in Hollywood? The adaptations, as I have already suggested, point away from themselves toward other possible kinds of adaptation: films that might build on Faulkner's adult insights and employ his Modernist structures. Since we are, however, in a decisively post-Modernist period, Godard's adaptive method may have more success here: to learn what we can from Faulkner's aesthetic, independent of his stories, and go on to explore and perhaps expand the range of verbal and visual signification in film.

Faulkner's screenplays did not have anything like the historical impact of his novels, although it is interesting to speculate what might have happened had *War Birds* been filmed and Faulkner been encouraged to write scripts the way he wrote fiction. The most important film with which he was directly associated, *The Big Sleep*, had most of its impact not because of Faulkner's contributions, but because of Hawks's and Furthman's last-minute revisions. A screenplay can be distinguished without being revolutionary, of course, and on the strength of *Today We Live* and *The Road to Glory*, among others, Faulkner has earned the right to be remembered as a good film dramatist.

The screenplays have further importance, simply as "works by Faulkner," and it is unfortunate that none of them except *The Big Sleep* and *The Southerner* has yet been published. In many cases his scripts illuminate, extend, and complicate the themes of his fiction. It is significant, for instance, that by the time he wrote *War Birds* he had already left the waste land of *Sartoris* in favor of the ethical renewal outlined in *The Unvanquished.* It is interesting that the version of "Spotted Horses" Faulkner published in 1931, before coming to Hollywood, has *less* "cutting" than the version he published in *The Hamlet* after he had been writing films for eight years;[9] one might have expected there to have been *more,* if the adages that Faulkner learned nothing from Hollywood and that the studios drained his experimental energy were true. *Turn About, Flying the Mail,* and *The Road to Glory* reveal Faulkner's continuing preoccupation with brother-sister relationships, outside any "Jefferson" context and free of any Gothic edge; I think it likely that one *could not* examine this theme in Faulkner's fiction without relating the discussion to these scripts.

One of the scenes Faulkner wrote into the final version of *Today We Live,* for example, is particularly significant because it summarizes the childhood sequences that Fitzgerald and Taylor had excised from *Turn About.* Those sequences—notably the "branch" episode that opened the screenplay—are closely related to *The Sound and the Fury,* and Faulkner evidently thought enough of those correspondences to make sure that *Today We Live* included two indirect references to his novel: the "say it again" scene between Ann and her brother, and the following dialogue, spoken by Claude:

> Oh, Ronnie—remember when we were tykes, messing about the brook and all? She said she would marry me—you remember, how we all said it, all three of us? And then when we were bigger, how we talked about it being in the chapel, with the padre, and the veils and wreaths, and the music of the voice that breathed o'er Eden—you remember. We were still children then, Ronnie. We're not children anymore—she's not, and I'm not. The chapel and padre seem a million miles away. There's no Eden anymore, and the wear is khaki, not veils. We didn't wait, Ronald.[10]

When Ronnie finds out that Claude has been sleeping with his sister, he says it is all right and kisses her. There is more to the incest theme, then, than Quentin's desire to kill himself and Caddy—or failing that, Dalton Ames. One of Quentin's crucial memories is of Caddy's running, veiled, to Benjy after her wedding:

> *That quick, her train caught up over her arm she ran out of the mirror like a cloud, her veil swirling in long glints her heels brittle and fast clutching her dress onto her shoulder with the other hand, running out of the mirror the smells roses roses the voice that breathed oe'r Eden.*[11]

John Keble's poem, "Holy Matrimony," was apparently sung at Caddy's wedding. It is a celebration of "the pure espousal / of Christian man and maid," and begins with the lines: "The voice that breathed o'er Eden, / That earliest wedding-day, / The primal marriage blessing, / It hath not passed away."[12] One of the essential differences between Quentin and his surrogates, Claude and Ronnie, is that Quentin is not willing to acknowledge that "there's no Eden anymore," no fall from innocence into anything but damnation and death. The ironic similarity among the three, however, is that all of them commit some version of suicide. This is only one example, and a fairly lightweight one, of the ways the screenplays can prove useful to students of Faulkner.

Most filmmaking is collaborative, and Faulkner did his best work alone. When he referred to film in his fiction, his tone was usually negative: it bears "germs" in *Pylon*, and is escapist with a vengeance in "Dry September." The story of Faulkner's film career is partly one of missed opportunities and hostility, but it is also a story of friendship and of dynamic creative exchange. If Faulkner felt it necessary at last to lock film and fiction into different "rooms," he has not by that decision bound those of us who admire and enjoy him to do the same.

NOTES

CHAPTER 1

[1] The only scholar to have read and thoroughly discussed most of Faulkner's screenplays appears to be George R. Sidney, whose Ph.D. thesis, *Faulkner in Hollywood* (Univ. of New Mexico, 1959), is acknowledged in Joseph Blotner's better-known essay, "Faulkner in Hollywood" [available in W. R. Robinson, *Man and the Movies* (Baltimore: Penguin, 1969)], and in Tom Dardis's recent study, *Some Time in the Sun* (New York: Scribner's, 1976). See ch. 4, note 1, below.

[2] See her lecture, "Portraits and Repetition," in *Gertrude Stein: Writings and Lectures, 1909–1945*, ed. Patricia Meyerowitz (Baltimore: Penguin, 1971), esp. p. 106.

[3] See Ezra Pound, *ABC of Reading* (New York: New Directions, 1960), pp. 21–22, and Sergei Eisenstein, *Film Form* (New York: Harcourt, Brace and World, 1949), pp. 29–30.

CHAPTER 2

[1] Ithaca: Cornell University Press, 1960.

[2] James Joyce, *Ulysses* (New York: Vintage, 1971), p. 176.

[3] William Faulkner, *The Sound and the Fury* (New York: Modern Library College Edition, n.d.), pp. 202–203.

[4] Wald *was* associated with some good films. He co-wrote *They Drive by Night*, and produced *Mildred Pierce* (on which Faulkner worked), *Key Largo, Sons and Lovers*, and most successfully *Peyton Place*. But experimental fiction was not his strong suit, although it was the focus of his vanity, and it is just as well that he never actually made his film of *Ulysses*.

[5] Reprinted in Sidney, *Faulkner in Hollywood*, pp. 242–244. Wald's articles on the same subject are on pp. 245–251.

CHAPTER 3

[1] *New York Herald Tribune*, May 6, 1933.

[2] Robert Littell in *The New Republic*, June 14, 1933.

[3] William Faulkner, *Pylon* (New York: Signet, 1968), p. 222.

[4] William Faulkner, *The Reivers* (New York: Random House, 1962), p. 19. This is the same Boon who figures in "The Bear."

[5] William Faulkner, *Knight's Gambit* (New York: Random House, 1949), p. 104.

CHAPTER 4

[1] At many points in this chapter, the information I provide contradicts previous scholarship. To avoid burdening the reader with excessive documentation, I have noted only the most significant points of difference. The pioneering study is George Sidney's Ph.D. thesis, *Faulkner in Hollywood* (1959; available through University Microfilms); its filmography is often inaccurate, and at least one of the screenplays described (*Slave Ship*) is apparently not the version on which Faulkner worked. Sidney's argument, however, is theoretically sound, and his practice of extensive quotation is very helpful. Joseph Blotner's *Faulkner: A Biography* (New York: Random House, 1974) provides much "hard" information on Faulkner's day-to-day life in Hollywood; I have followed Blotner wherever he is not contradicted by my primary sources, which are the screenplays themselves, the films, and the studio files. Tom Dardis's *Some Time in the Sun* (New York: Scribner's, 1976) relies heavily on both Blotner and Sidney, as well as on interviews with Faulkner's co-workers; unfortunately, it passes on many of their errors, and is not a reliable source. (For example: the death scene Faulkner wrote for *Air Force* is not mentioned by Sidney; Blotner describes it as occurring near the end of the film, and Dardis not only calls it the film's closing scene but refers to the "final chords" of the score. The scene actually occurs two-thirds of the way through the

film, and the subdued music imitates a warming engine.) Some of my information comes from a long talk I had with Howard Hawks in May, 1976; I have passed on his stories only when they checked out (which they often did not).

[2] For a complete list of Faulkner's writings for film and television, see the filmography at the end of this book.

[3] Faulkner said as much himself. See Blotner, p. 773.

[4] For a description of *Manservant*, see Blotner, p. 774.

[5] This has led to some confusion as to whether Faulkner worked on the Behn/Furthman project, *Honor* (from Faulkner's story of the same name), or was simply working on *War Birds* under that title.

[6] Actually this is not a flashback but a mindscreen, since the past is being presented not "as it happened" but "as John tells it." It should be noted, in any case, that *War Birds* is one of the few scripts in which Faulkner juggled with time.

[7] This ending was apparently inspired by Abel Gance's film *J'Accuse*, which features a parade of ghost soldiers. The irony is that although Gance's actors too were genuine soldiers, *they* were simply *on leave* when the picture was shot. Many of them died in combat before *J'Accuse* was released in 1919.

[8] (Paris: Gallimard, 1949; New York: Pantheon, 1954). For an extension of this discussion, see Bruce Kawin, *Telling It Again and Again: Repetition in Literature and Film* (Ithaca: Cornell University Press, 1972).

[9] I have been unable to establish who wrote these lines. My best guess is that Sayre or Johnson wrote the scene (possibly from Faulkner's notes for the first temporary screenplay—a discarded scene?) for the *Zero Hour* draft in which it first appears, and that Faulkner selected and rewrote it when he and Hawks assembled the shooting script. This dialogue is taken from the screen.

[10] For two marvelous, dense excerpts from Faulkner's *Banjo on My Knee*, see Sidney, pp. 161–165. For the complete

Drums along the Mohawk treatment, see Sidney, pp. 113–151. *Slave Ship* clearly bears Johnson's stamp, although Faulkner may been responsible for the device of the repeated "curse" pronounced on the *Albatross*. Johnson is one of Hollywood's finest screenwriters; in both dialogue and structure his work is entertaining, powerful, and clear. Without depending on the pretentious gestures of a Dudley Nichols, he achieves the genuine, the moving, and at times the complex, but never at the sacrifice of lucidity. His dislike of Faulkner's screenwriting proceeded mainly from its willful involutedness. Johnson's best screenplays include *The House of Rothschild, The Prisoner of Shark Island, Jesse James, The Grapes of Wrath, Chad Hanna, Tobacco Road, The Dark Mirror, The Three Faces of Eve, The World of Henry Orient,* and much of *The Southerner* and *The Road to Glory*. His latest is *The Dirty Dozen.*

[11] For a synopsis of *Country Lawyer*, see Sidney, pp. 167–184. *Battle Cry* also bears some similarity to *Go Down, Moses,* though neither screenplay approaches that novel in any but a thematic sense.

[12] According to Leigh Brackett; see Donald Chase, *Filmmaking: The Collaborative Art*, ed. James Powers (Boston: Little, Brown/American Film Institute, 1975), pp. 54–55.

[13] It is this version of the screenplay that has been published in *Film Scripts One*, ed. Garrett, Hardison, and Gelfman (New York: Appleton-Century-Crofts, 1971; distributed by Irvington Publishers), pp. 137–329. The final, amended shooting script, with Furthman's and Hawks's contributions, is on file in the UCLA Theatre Arts Library and at Warner's.

[14] In the film it is suggested but not proved that Joe Brody killed the chauffeur. Chandler's remark to Hawks that "the butler did it" was a joke.

[15] Faulkner's scenes between Marlowe and General Sternwood make much of the question of heartbreak. Hawks revised and cut these so that the one remaining scene is very close to Chandler's original (except for the detail of Marlowe's friendship with Regan).

[16] *Film Scripts One*, pp. 266–267.

[17] Blotner, p. 1184. Note, however, that Blotner has Faulkner working on *The Southerner* several months after the picture's Los Angeles release.

[18] Blotner, p. 1190. Faulkner's personal copy was donated by Longstreet to the University of Virginia's Alderman Library.

[19] Dialogue taken from the shooting script (September, 1954), pp. 7–8.

CHAPTER 5

[1] At this point the parallel with King David enlarges to include William Shakespeare, a small-town boy who used his London earnings to establish New Place, and whose children included the twins, Hamnet and Judith. (Hamnet's death is presumed to have been one of the precipitators of *Hamlet.*) The third crucial parallel is with King Agamemnon, who sacrificed his daughter, Iphigenia, so that his "design" (the Trojan War) would succeed. Faulkner calls attention to all this by naming Sutpen's half-black daughter Clytemnestra (the name of Agamemnon's wife); by linking Henry/Hamnet with Quentin/Hamlet; and by referring in the novel's title to David's cry of remorse upon learning that *his* design has resulted in the death of his son, Absalom. Much of the novel's point is that Sutpen never utters anything like the cry: "Would I had died for thee, O Absalom, my son, my son!" The Henry/Judith story connects with the Quentin/Caddy story, as well as with that of Absalom, Amnon, and Tamar (see II Samuel, chapters 13–19). The final connection, which is with Orestes and Electra, was probably suggested by O'Neill's 1931 play, *Mourning Becomes Electra,* in which the Civil and Trojan wars are symbolically interrelated, and which it is extremely likely that Faulkner saw.

[2] Letter to Malcolm Cowley in 1944, reprinted in *The Faulkner-Cowley File* (New York: Viking Press, 1966), pp. 14–17. In this same letter he says that he has finally managed to "work at Hollywood 6 months, stay at home 6, am used to it now and have movie work locked off into another room."

[3] Blotner, p. 854; Dardis, p. 127.

[4] All quotations from *Revolt in the Earth* are by permission of the University of Virginia's Alderman Library, which has what is apparently the only extant copy.

[5] "Wash," in *Collected Stories of William Faulkner* (New York: Random House, 1950), p. 542.

[6] Sutpen may be the biological parent; it is likely but not clear.

[7] House telegram; January 6, 1943.

[8] Blotner, p. 1197.

CHAPTER 6

[1] Jean-Luc Godard, *Godard on Godard*, ed. Jean Narboni and Tom Milne (New York: Viking Press, 1972), p. 29; see also pp. 175 and 234 .

[2] Jean-Paul Sartre, "On *The Sound and the Fury*: Time in the Work of Faulkner," *Situations I*; reprinted in Sartre, *Literary and Philosophical Essays*, trans. Annette Michelson (London: Rider & Co., 1955), pp. 79–87.

[3] See Magny's *The Age of the American Novel: The Film Aesthetic of Fiction Between the Two Wars*, trans. Eleanor Hochman (New York: Ungar, 1972), and Maurice Coindreau, *The Time of William Faulkner* (Columbia: University of South Carolina Press, 1971).

[4] Eric Rhode, *A History of the Cinema from its Origins to 1970* (New York: Hill and Wang, 1976), p. 534. See also Georges Sadoul, *Dictionary of Films*, trans. Peter Morris (Berkeley: University of California Press, 1972), pp. 287–288.

[5] Alain Robbe-Grillet, *For a New Novel*, trans. Richard Howard (New York: Grove Press, 1965), pp. 26, 33, 137, 139, 149–156. For a brilliant use of montage in fiction, see the climax of Robbe-Grillet's novel *Jealousy*—in many ways the culmination of the line of argument pursued in this study; *Two Novels*

by Robbe-Grillet, trans. Richard Howard (New York: Grove Press, 1965), pp. 112–114.

[6] Marianne Moore, "Poetry" (1921 version).

[7] Godard, pp. 29–30. The essay was written in 1952.

[8] Richard Roud, *Jean-Luc Godard* (Bloomington: Indiana University Press, 1970), p. 101; see also p. 49.

[9] Sidney, p. 220.

[10] Dialogue taken from the screen.

[11] William Faulkner, *The Sound and the Fury* (New York: Modern Library College Edition, n.d.), p. 100. See also p. 130. The italics are Faulkner's.

[12] *The Home Book of Verse* (New York: Holt, 1922), p. 1197.

FAULKNER FILMOGRAPHY

[Unless otherwise stated, all works are by Faulkner. For works that changed title during composition or production, all known titles are given, although discussion is restricted to those scripts on which Faulkner worked. Where a single date is given, it is either that of completion or that on which the script was copied by the story department.]

1. MANSERVANT
Treatment (21 pp.), based on Faulkner's story "Love."
May 25, 1932 MGM

2. THE COLLEGE WIDOW
Treatment (13 pp.).
May 26, 1932 MGM

3. ABSOLUTION
Treatment (9 pp.), marginally based on Faulkner's story "All the Dead Pilots."
June 1, 1932 MGM

4. FLYING THE MAIL
Treatment (16 pp.), based on an original story and treatment by Ralph Graves and Bernard Fineman.
June 3, 1932 MGM

5. TURN TO THE RIGHT
(Assigned to the project; no evidence he wrote anything.)
June, 1932 MGM

6. TODAY WE LIVE/TURN ABOUT
TURN ABOUT, treatment by Faulkner, based on his story "Turn About."
Early July, 1932 MGM

Note: Portions of this Filmography have appeared in *Film Quarterly*.

TURN ABOUT, screenplay (122 pp.) by Faulkner but signed by Faulkner and Hawks.
August 24, 1932

TODAY WE LIVE, screenplay by Edith Fitzgerald and Dwight Taylor, closely based on the second half of Faulkner's screenplay; additional dialogue by Faulkner.
November 28, 1932

TODAY WE LIVE released March 3, 1933, by MGM.

Credits: Produced [Prod] and Directed [Dir] by Howard Hawks; Photographed [Ph] by Oliver T. Marsh; Edited [Ed] by Edward Curtis; Screenplay [Scr] by Edith Fitzgerald and Dwight Taylor; Story and Dialogue by Faulkner; Starring [St] Joan Crawford (Diana Boyce-Smith), Gary Cooper (Richard Bogard), Robert Young (Claude Hope), Franchot Tone (Ronnie Boyce-Smith), Roscoe Karns (McGinnis), Louise Closser Hale (Applegate).

7. WAR BIRDS

FAULKNER STORY #2, treatment, based on Faulkner's stories "Ad Astra" and "All the Dead Pilots," and marginally on the novel *Sartoris* (*Flags in the Dust*), as well as on the novel he had been assigned to adapt: *Diary of the Unknown Aviator* by John McGavock Grider (on which MGM had been working since 1926 under the titles *Honor* and *War Birds* — and on which Faulkner may have based "Ad Astra" in the first place).
1932 MGM

WAR BIRDS, screenplay (143 pp.).
December, 1932–January 12, 1933 (possibly revised March, 1933)

8. HONOR

Treatment by Harry Behn, based on Faulkner's story "Honor."
January, 1933 MGM

Screenplay (107 pp.) by Behn, Jules Furthman, and possibly Faulkner.
March 30, 1933 (revised May 10, 1933)

9. MYTHICAL LATIN-AMERICAN KINGDOM STORY (working title)
Screenplay (110 pp.).
Late March–August 26, 1933 MGM

10. LAZY RIVER/BRIDE OF THE BAYOU/IN OLD LOUISIANA/LOUISIANA LOU
Screenplay by Lucien Hubbard, based on the play *Ruby* by Lea David Freeman.
Faulkner worked on dialogue during shooting.
April 26–May 13, 1933 MGM
LAZY RIVER released March 7, 1934, by MGM.
Credits: Prod: Lucien Hubbard; Dir: George B. Seitz; Scr: Hubbard; St: Jean Parker (Sarah), Robert Young (Bill Drexel), Ted Healy (Gabby), Nat Pendleton (Tiny), C. Henry Gordon (Sam Kee).

11. SUTTER'S GOLD
Treatment by Sergei Eisenstein (assisted by Ivor Montagu and G. V. Alexandrov), based on the biography *L'Or* by Blaise Cendrars.
1930 PARAMOUNT
Treatment (107 pp.).
July, 1934 UNIVERSAL (for Hawks)
SUTTER'S GOLD released March, 1936, by Universal.
Credits: Prod: Edmund Grainger; Dir: James Cruze; Scr: Jack Kirkland, Walter Woods, and George O'Neill, based on *L'Or* and on a story by Bruno Frank; St: Edward Arnold (Sutter), Lee Tracy (Pete Perkin), Binnie Barnes (Countess Bartoffski), Katharine Alexander (Anna Sutter), Harry Carey (Kit Carson), Billy Gilbert (Gen. Ramos).

12. THE ROAD TO GLORY/WOODEN CROSSES/ZERO HOUR

LES CROIX DE BOIS (1932), film directed by Raymond Bernard, based on the novel of the same name by Roland Dorgelès.

WOODEN CROSSES, screenplay (170 pp.) by Faulkner and Joel Sayre, based on the film *Les Croix de bois* and on a story Howard Hawks developed from the wartime experiences of a soldier he met in Paris.
December 16–31, 1935 20TH CENTURY-FOX

Revised story outline by Nunnally Johnson, incorporating changes suggested by Darryl F. Zanuck.
January 10, 1936

WOODEN CROSSES, first temporary screenplay by Sayre and Johnson.
January 14, 1936

WOODEN CROSSES, first final screenplay by Sayre and Johnson, incorporating further Zanuck changes.
January 24, 1936

WOODEN CROSSES, second final screenplay by Sayre and Johnson.
January 27, 1936

ZERO HOUR, third final screenplay (135 pp.) by Sayre and Johnson; closest to the film as shot.
January 27, 1936 (revised January 29, 1936)

New scenes written in April, 1936, presumably by Faulkner and Hawks. As shot, THE ROAD TO GLORY is a composite of all the above scripts.

THE ROAD TO GLORY released June 2, 1936, by 20th Century-Fox.

Credits: Prod: Darryl F. Zanuck; Assoc. Prod: Nunnally Johnson; Dir: Howard Hawks; Ph: Gregg Toland; Ed: Edward Curtis; Scr: Joel Sayre and William Faulkner; St: Fredric March (Lt. Michel Denet), Warner Baxter (Capt. Paul LaRoche), Lionel Barrymore (Papa LaRoche), June Lang (Monique), Gregory Ratoff (Bouffiou), Victor Kilian (Regnier).

13. BANJO ON MY KNEE

Treatment (32 pp.) of the fifth and sixth sequences in a

collaborative treatment coordinated by Nunnally Johnson and based on the novel *Banjo on My Knee* by Harry Hamilton.

February–March, 1936 20TH CENTURY-FOX

Revised treatment (44 pp.) of fifth and sixth sequences.

March, 1936

Screenplay by Francis Edwards Faragoh, based loosely on the collaborative treatment.

May 15, 1936

Screenplay by Nunnally Johnson, discarding most of the above.

June 19, 1936

Final screenplay by Johnson.

August 18, 1936

BANJO ON MY KNEE released November, 1936, by 20th Century-Fox.

Credits: Prod: Darryl F. Zanuck; Assoc. Prod. and Scr: Nunnally Johnson; Dir: John Cromwell; St: Barbara Stanwyck (Pearl), Joel McCrea (Ernie Holley), Walter Brennan (Newt Holley), Buddy Ebsen (Buddy), Helen Westley (Grandma), Walter Catlett (Warfield Scott), Katharine de Mille (Leota Long), Victor Kilian (Slade), Anthony Martin (Chick Bean), Minna Gombell (Ruby), and the Hall Johnson Choir.

14. GUNGA DIN

Treatment and dialogue revision.

March–April, 1936 RKO

GUNGA DIN released January, 1939, by RKO.

Credits: Prod. and Dir: George Stevens; Scr: Joel Sayre and Fred Guiol; Story: Ben Hecht and Charles MacArthur, based on the poem "Gunga Din" by Rudyard Kipling; St: Cary Grant (Cutter), Victor McLaglen (MacChesney), Douglas Fairbanks, Jr. (Ballantine), Sam Jaffe (Gunga Din), Eduardo Ciannelli (Sufi Khan), Joan Fontaine (Emmy).

15. SLAVE SHIP/THE LAST SLAVER

THE LAST SLAVER, screenplay by Sam Hellman and

Gladys Lehman, based on the novel *The Last Slaver* by George S. King.
June 22, 1936

THE LAST SLAVER, temporary screenplay by Faulkner and Nunnally Johnson, based on the above screenplay and incorporating changes suggested by Zanuck.
August–September, 1936 20TH CENTURY-FOX

THE LAST SLAVER, revised final screenplay by Johnson.
December 15, 1936

SLAVE SHIP released June, 1937, by 20th Century-Fox.

Credits: Prod: Darryl F. Zanuck; Assoc. Prod: Nunnally Johnson; Dir: Tay Garnett; Ph: Ernest Palmer; Ed: Lloyd Nosler; Scr: Sam Hellman, Lamar Trotti, and Gladys Lehman; Story: William Faulkner; St: Warner Baxter (Jim Lovett), Wallace Beery (Jack Thompson), Elizabeth Allan (Nancy Marlowe), Mickey Rooney (Swifty), George Sanders (Lefty), Jane Darwell (Mrs. Marlowe), Joseph Schildkraut (Danelo), and the Hall Johnson Choir.

16. FOUR MEN AND A PRAYER

Comments and minor revisions on a treatment by Sonya Levien and Wallace Sullivan, based on the novel *Four Men and a Prayer* by David Garth.
September 1–2, 1936 20TH CENTURY-FOX

FOUR MEN AND A PRAYER released April 29, 1938, by 20th Century-Fox.

Credits: Prod: Kenneth MacGowan; Dir: John Ford; Scr: Richard Sherman, Sonya Levien, and Walter Ferris; St: Loretta Young (Lynn), Richard Greene (Geoff), George Sanders (Wyatt), David Niven (Chris), C. Aubrey Smith (Leigh), William Henry (Rod).

17. SUBMARINE PATROL/SPLINTER FLEET

SPLINTER FLEET, screenplay (129 pp.) by Faulkner and Kathryn Scola, based on the novel *The Splinter Fleet of the Otranto Barrage* by Ray Millholland.

September 4–November 30, 1936 20TH CENTURY-FOX

SUBMARINE PATROL released November 25, 1938, by 20th Century-Fox.

Credits: Prod: Darryl F. Zanuck; Assoc. Prod: Gene Markey; Dir: John Ford; Scr: Rian James, Darrell Ware, and Jack Yellen; St: Richard Greene (Perry Townsend), Nancy Kelly (Susan Leeds), Preston Foster (Lt. Drake), George Bancroft (Capt. Leeds), Slim Summerville (Spuds), John Carradine (McAllison), Joan Valerie (Anne), Maxie Rosenbloom (Joe Duffy), Ward Bond (Olaf), Elisha Cook, Jr. (Professor).

18. DANCE HALL/THE GIANT SWING/THE BOUNCER AND THE LADY

Minor contributions to a screenplay by Kathryn Scola and Lamar Trotti, based on the novel *The Giant Swing* by William Riley Burnett.

March 9–11, 1937 20TH CENTURY-FOX

DANCE HALL released June, 1941, by 20th Century-Fox

Credits: Prod: Sol M. Wurtzel; Dir: Irving Pichel; Scr: Stanley Rauh and Ethel Hill; St: Cesar Romero (Duke McKay), Carole Landis (Lily Brown), Willian Henry (Joe Brooks), June Storey (Ada), J. Edward Bromberg (Max Brandon).

19. DRUMS ALONG THE MOHAWK

Treatment (26 pp.), based on the novel *Drums Along the Mohawk* by Walter D. Edmonds.

March, 1937 20TH CENTURY-FOX

Screenplay (238 pp.), unsigned but possibly by Faulkner.

July 3, 1937

Final screenplay by Lamar Trotti, based on treatments by Sonya Levien and Walter Edmonds.

April–May, 1939

DRUMS ALONG THE MOHAWK released November, 1939, by 20th Century-Fox.

Credits: Prod: Darryl F. Zanuck; Dir: John Ford; Scr: Lamar Trotti and Sonya Levien; St: Claudette Colbert (Lana Martin), Henry Fonda (Gilbert Martin), Edna May Oliver (Mrs. McKlennar), Eddie Collins (Christian Reall), John Carradine (Caldwell), Dorris Bowden (Mary Reall), Ward Bond (Adam Helmer), Chief Big Tree (Blue Back), Robert Lowery (John Weaver), Arthur Shields (Rev. Rosenkrantz), Roger Imhof (Gen. Herkimer).

20. THE DE GAULLE STORY

Screenplay (153 pp.).

July–November, 1942 (revised March, 1943)

WARNER BROS.

21. AIR FORCE

Faulkner rewrote two scenes in a screenplay by Dudley Nichols.

September, 1942 WARNER BROS.

AIR FORCE released March 20, 1943, by Warner Bros.

Credits: Prod: Hal B. Wallis; Dir: Howard Hawks; Ph: James Wong Howe, Elmer Dyer, and Charles Marshall; Ed: George Amy; Scr: Dudley Nichols; St: B-17 No. 05564 (*Mary-Ann*), John Ridgely (Capt. Quincannon), John Garfield (Sgt. Winocki), Harry Carey (Sgt. White), George Tobias (Corp. Weinberg), James Brown (Lt. Rader), Gig Young (Lt. Williams), Arthur Kennedy (Lt. McMartin), Charles Drake (Lt. Hauser), Ward Wood (Corp. Peterson).

22. REVOLT IN THE EARTH

Screenplay (62 pp.) by Faulkner and Dudley Murphy, based on Faulkner's novel *Absalom, Absalom!*, and his story "Wash."

Late 1942

23. THE LIFE AND DEATH OF A BOMBER/LIBERATOR STORY
Treatment.
November, 1942–January 23, 1943 WARNER BROS.

24. BACKGROUND TO DANGER
Faulkner, A. I. Bezzerides, and Daniel Fuchs made minor revisions on a screenplay by W. R. Burnett, based on the novel *Uncommon Danger* by Eric Ambler.
November 23–December 7, 1942 WARNER BROS.
BACKGROUND TO DANGER released June, 1943, by Warner Bros.
Credits: Prod: Jerry Wald; Dir: Raoul Walsh; Scr: W. R. Burnett; St: George Raft (Joe Barton), Brenda Marshall (Tamara), Sydney Greenstreet (Col. Robinson), Peter Lorre (Zaloshoff), Osa Massen (Ana Remzi), Turhan Bey (Hassen).

25. NORTHERN PURSUIT/TO THE LAST MAN/FIVE THOUSAND TROJAN HORSES
Screenplay by Faulkner, A. I. Bezzerides, Robert Rossen, Frank Gruber, and others, based on the story "Five Thousand Trojan Horses" by Leslie T. White.
February, 1943 WARNER BROS.
NORTHERN PURSUIT released November, 1943, by Warner Bros.
Credits: Prod: Jack Chertok; Dir: Raoul Walsh; Scr: A. I. Bezzerides; St: Errol Flynn (Steve Wagner), Julie Bishop (Laura McBain), Helmut Dantine (Hugo Von Keller), John Ridgely (Jim Austen), Gene Lockhart (Ernst), Monte Blue (Jean).

26. DEEP VALLEY
Continuity and dialogue (38 pp.), based on the novel *Deep Valley* by Dan Totheroh.
March, 1943 WARNER BROS.
DEEP VALLEY released August, 1947, by Warner Bros.
Credits: Prod: Henry Blanke; Dir: Jean Negulesco; Scr:

Salka Viertel and Stephen Morehouse Avery; St: Ida Lupino (Libby), Dane Clark (Barry), Wayne Morris (Barker), Fay Bainter (Mrs. Saul), Henry Hull (Mr. Saul), Willard Robertson (Sheriff).

27. COUNTRY LAWYER

Treatment (52 pp.), marginally based on the family chronicle *Country Lawyer* by Bellamy Partridge.
March, 1943 WARNER BROS.

28. BATTLE CRY

Treatment by Faulkner and Howard Hawks.
April, 1943 WARNER BROS.
First temporary screenplay (140 pp.).
April 21, 1943
Second temporary screenplay (231 pp.).
June, 1943
Third temporary screenplay, by Faulkner and Steve Fisher.
June 21, 1943
Revision of French and Russian sequences (117 pp.).
July, 1943

29. WHO?

Treatment (51 pp.) based on an idea by Henry Hathaway and William Bacher. (Eventually, this became the novel *A Fable*.)
September–November, 1943

30. TO HAVE AND HAVE NOT

Treatment by Howard Hawks and Ernest Hemingway, based on the novel *To Have and Have Not* by Hemingway.
Screenplay by Faulkner and Jules Furthman.
February, 1944 WARNER BROS.
Revisions by Faulkner, Furthman, Hawks, and "Stuttering Sam."
March–May, 1944
TO HAVE AND HAVE NOT released October 11, 1944, by Warner Bros.

Credits: Prod. and Dir: Howard Hawks; Ph: Sidney Hickox; Ed: Christian Nyby; Scr: Jules Furthman and William Faulkner; St: Humphrey Bogart (Harry Morgan/Steve), Lauren Bacall (Marie/Slim), Walter Brennan (Eddie), Hoagy Carmichael (Crickett), Dan Seymour (Capt. Renard), Marcel Dalio (Frenchie), Walter Sande (Johnson).

31. GOD IS MY CO-PILOT

Treatment (15 pp.) based on the autobiography *God Is My Co-Pilot* by Col. Robert Lee Scott.

February and August, 1944 WARNER BROS.

GOD IS MY CO-PILOT released March, 1945, by Warner Bros.

Credits: Prod: Robert Buckner; Dir: Robert Florey; Scr: Peter Milne; St: Dennis Morgan (Col. Scott), Dane Clark (Johnny), Raymond Massey (Gen. Chennault), Alan Hale (Big Mike), Andrea King (Catherine), John Ridgely (Tex Hill), Richard Loo (Tokyo Joe).

32. THE DAMNED DON'T CRY

Treatment based on a story by Gertrude Walker and on Faulkner's own story, "The Brooch."

May–June, 1944 WARNER BROS.

THE DAMNED DON'T CRY released April, 1950, by Warner Bros.

Credits: Prod: Jerry Wald; Dir: Vincent Sherman; Scr: Harold Medford and Jerome Weidman; St: Joan Crawford (Ethel Whitehead), David Brian (George Castleman), Steve Cochran (Nick Prenta), Kent Smith (Martin Blackford).

33. THE ADVENTURES OF DON JUAN

Faulkner revised a screenplay based on a story by Herbert Dalmas.

June, 1944 WARNER BROS.

THE ADVENTURES OF DON JUAN released December, 1945, by Warner Bros.

Credits: Prod: Jerry Wald; Dir: Vincent Sherman; Scr:

George Oppenheimer and Harry Kurnitz; St. Errol Flynn (Don Juan), Viveca Lindfors (Queen Margaret), Robert Douglas (Duke de Lorca), Alan Hale (Leporello).

34. FOG OVER LONDON/THE AMAZING DR. CLITTERHOUSE

THE AMAZING DR. CLITTERHOUSE (1938), film directed by Anatole Litvak, based on the play of the same name by Barré Lyndon; screenplay by John Huston and John Wexley.

FOG OVER LONDON, treatment for a remake of the above.
July, 1944 WARNER BROS.

FOG OVER LONDON, second treatment.
August, 1944

35. ESCAPE IN THE DESERT/STRANGERS IN OUR MIDST/THE PETRIFIED FOREST

THE PETRIFIED FOREST (1936), film directed by Archie Mayo, based on the play of the same name by Robert Sherwood.

STRANGERS IN OUR MIDST, screenplay by Faulkner and A. I. Bezzerides, based marginally on the above.
July–August, 1944 WARNER BROS.

ESCAPE IN THE DESERT released May, 1945, by Warner Bros.

Credits: Prod: Alex Gottlieb; Dir: Edward A. Blatt; Scr: Thomas Job, based on Marvin Borowsky's adaptation of Sherwood's play; St: Philip Dorn (Philip Artveld), Helmut Dantine (Capt. Becker), Jean Sullivan (Jane), Alan Hale (Dr. Orville Tedder), Irene Manning (Mrs. Lora Tedder), Samuel S. Hinds (Gramp).

36. THE SOUTHERNER

Screenplay by Jean Renoir and Nunnally Johnson, based on Hugo Butler's adaptation of the novel *Hold Autumn in Your Hand* by George Sessions Perry.

1944 PRODUCING ARTISTS

Final screenplay by Faulkner and Renoir.
Perhaps Summer, 1944

THE SOUTHERNER released April 30, 1945, by United Artists.

Credits: Prod: David L. Loew and Robert Hakim; Dir. and Scr: Jean Renoir; Ph: Lucien Andriot; Ed: Gregg Tallas; St: Zachary Scott (Sam Tucker), Betty Field (Nona Tucker), J. Carrol Naish (Henry Devers), Beulah Bondi (Grandma), Charles Kemper (Tim).

37. THE BIG SLEEP

Screenplay (172 pp.) by Faulkner and Leigh Brackett, based on the novel *The Big Sleep* by Raymond Chandler.
August–September, 1944 WARNER BROS.

Final screenplay by Faulkner and Brackett.
October 26, 1944

Minor revisions by Faulkner and "Stuttering Sam"; major revisions by Jules Furthman and Howard Hawks.
December, 1944–March, 1945

THE BIG SLEEP released August, 1946, by Warner Bros.

Credits: Prod. and Dir: Howard Hawks; Ph: Sidney Hickox; Ed: Christian Nyby; Scr: William Faulkner, Leigh Brackett, and Jules Furthman; St: Humphrey Bogart (Philip Marlowe), Lauren Bacall (Vivian Sternwood), John Ridgely (Eddie Mars), Martha Vickers (Carmen Sternwood), Dorothy Malone (Bookshop Girl), Charles Waldren (Gen. Sternwood), Elisha Cook, Jr. (Jones), Bob Steele (Canino), Sonia Darrin (Agnes), Louis Jean Heydt (Joe Brody).

38. MILDRED PIERCE

Faulkner revised a screenplay based on the novel *Mildred Pierce* by James M. Cain.
November, 1944 WARNER BROS.

MILDRED PIERCE released September, 1945, by Warner Bros.
Credits: Prod: Jerry Wald; Dir: Michael Curtiz; Scr: Ranald MacDougall and Catherine Turney; St: Joan Crawford (Mildred Pierce), Jack Carson (Wally), Zachary Scott (Monty Beragon), Eve Arden (Ida), Bruce Bennett (Bert Pierce), Ann Blyth (Veda Pierce).

39. BARN BURNING
Treatment (50 pp.) by Faulkner and A. I. Bezzerides, based on Faulkner's story "Barn Burning."
Summer, 1945

40. STALLION ROAD
Treatment (17 pp.) based on the novel *Stallion Road* by Stephen Longstreet.
June, 1945 WARNER BROS.
First temporary screenplay (134 pp.).
June–July, 1945
Second temporary screenplay (151 pp.).
August, 1945
Final screenplay by Stephen Longstreet, in admiration but not imitation of Faulkner's version.
STALLION ROAD released April, 1947, by Warner Bros.
Credits: Prod: Alex Gottlieb; Dir: James V. Kern; Scr: Stephen Longstreet; St: Ronald Reagan (Larry Hanrahan), Alexis Smith (Rory Teller), Zachary Scott (Stephen Purcell), Peggy Knudsen (Daisy Otis).

41. CONTINUOUS PERFORMANCE
Treatment (38 pp.) by Faulkner and an unnamed collaborator.
Early 1946

42. ONE WAY TO CATCH A HORSE
Treatment (36 pp.).
No date; perhaps 1946

43. DREADFUL HOLLOW
Screenplay (159 pp.).
No date; probably 1940s (for Hawks)

44. INTRUDER IN THE DUST
Faulkner looked over and partially revised a screenplay by Ben Maddow, based on Faulkner's novel *Intruder in the Dust*.
February, 1949 MGM
INTRUDER IN THE DUST released November 22, 1949, by MGM.
Credits: Prod. and Dir: Clarence Brown; Ph: Robert Surtees; Ed: Robert J. Kern; Scr: Ben Maddow; St: Juano Hernandez (Lucas Beauchamp), David Brian (John Gavin Stevens), Claude Jarman, Jr. (Chick Mallison), Elizabeth Patterson (Eunice Habersham), Porter Hall (Nub Gowrie), Will Geer (Sheriff Hampton), Charles Kemper (Crawford Gowrie), Elzie Emanuel (Aleck Sander), David Clarke (Vinson Gowrie).

45. THE LEFT HAND OF GOD
Screenplay based on the novel *The Left Hand of God* by William E. Barrett.
February–March, 1951 WARNER BROS. (for Hawks)
THE LEFT HAND OF GOD released September, 1955, by 20th Century-Fox.
Credits: Prod: Buddy Adler; Dir: Edward Dmytryk; Scr: Alfred Hayes; St: Humphrey Bogart (James Carmondy/Father O'Shea), Gene Tierney (Ann Scott), Lee J. Cobb (Lieh Yang), Agnes Moorehead (Beryl Sigman), E. G. Marshall (Dr. Sigman).

46. (TV) THE BROOCH
Teleplay, based on Faulkner's story "The Brooch."
March, 1953 CBS
Final teleplay by Faulkner, Ed Rice, and Richard McDonagh.
March, 1953

THE BROOCH broadcast on *Lux Video Theatre*, April 2, 1953.

47. (TV) SHALL NOT PERISH

Teleplay, based on Faulkner's story "Shall Not Perish." April, 1953 CBS

SHALL NOT PERISH broadcast on *Lux Video Theatre*, February 11, 1954.

48. (TV) OLD MAN

Treatment (42 pp.) based on the "Old Man" sections of Faulkner's novel *The Wild Palms*.
April, 1953

49. LAND OF THE PHARAOHS

Screenplay by Faulkner, Howard Hawks, Harry Kurnitz, and probably Harold Jack Bloom.
December, 1953–March, 1954 WARNER BROS.

Final screenplay (122 pp.) by Hawks and Kurnitz; minor revision of the above.
September 28, 1954

LAND OF THE PHARAOHS released July 2, 1955, by Warner Bros.

Credits: Prod. and Dir: Howard Hawks; Ph: Lee Garmes and Russell Harlan; Ed: V. Sagovsky; Scr: William Faulkner, Harry Kurnitz, and Harold Jack Bloom; St: Jack Hawkins (Khufu, the Pharaoh), Joan Collins (Princess Nellifer), Alexis Minotis (Hamar), James Robertson Justice (Vashtar), Dewey Martin (Senta), Sydney Chaplin (Treneh), Kerima (Queen Nailla), Luisa Boni (Kyra), Piero Giagnoli (Prince Zanin).

50. (TV) THE GRADUATION DRESS

Teleplay by Faulkner and Joan Williams.
No date; probably late 1950s CBS

THE GRADUATION DRESS broadcast on *General Electric Theatre*, October 30, 1960.

[Note: The University of Virginia's Alderman Library has three untitled and undated manuscripts not included above:]

51. UNTITLED SCIENCE-FICTION SCENARIO (2 pp.)
(Characters: Zweistein and Dale; perhaps 1948.)

52. UNTITLED SCRIPT (32 pp.)
(Characters: Sarastro, Anna, Rico, and David; perhaps early 1940s.)

53. UNTITLED TELEVISION SERIES (6 pp.)
(Typed on verso of pages from *The Mansion*; late 1950s.)

SELECTED BIBLIOGRAPHY

Antrim, Harry. "Faulkner's Suspended Style." *University Review*, Winter, 1965.

Beck, Warren. *Man in Motion: Faulkner's Trilogy*. Madison: University of Wisconsin Press, 1961.

Blotner, Joseph. *Faulkner: A Biography*. New York: Random House, 1974.

Brooks, Cleanth. *William Faulkner: The Yoknapatawpha Country*. New Haven: Yale University Press, 1966.

Chase, Donald and James Powers, eds. *Filmmaking: The Collaborative Art*. Boston: Little, Brown and Co./American Film Institute, 1975.

Coindreau, Maurice. *The Time of William Faulkner*. Columbia: University of South Carolina Press, 1971.

Cowley, Malcolm. *The Faulkner-Cowley File: Letters and Memories, 1944–1962*. New York: Viking Press, 1966.

Eidsvik, Charles. "Demonstrating Film Influence." *Literature/Film Quarterly*, April, 1973.

Eisenstein, Sergei. *Film Form*, trans. Jay Leyda. New York: Harcourt, Brace, and World, 1949.

Fadiman, Regina K. *Faulkner's "Intruder in the Dust": Novel into Film*. Knoxville: University of Tennessee Press, 1977.

Gwynn, Frederick and Joseph Blotner, eds. *Faulkner in the University: Class Conferences at the University of Virginia, 1957–1958*. Charlottesville: University of Virginia Press, 1959.

Kawin, Bruce. *Telling It Again and Again: Repetition in Literature and Film*. Ithaca: Cornell University Press, 1972.

Kazula, Irene. "William Faulkner's Subjective Style." *Kwartalnik Neofilologiczny* (Warsaw), 1964.

Magny, Claude-Edmonde. *The Age of the American Novel: The Film Aesthetic of Fiction between the Two Wars*, trans. Eleanor Hochman. New York: Ungar, 1972.

Meriwether, James. *The Literary Career of William Faulkner: A Bibliographical Study*. Princeton: Princeton University Press, 1961.

———. "William Faulkner," in Jackson Bryer, ed., *Sixteen Modern American Authors: A Survey of Research and Criticism.* New York: W. W. Norton and Co., 1973.

Reed, Joseph. *Faulkner's Narrative.* New Haven: Yale University Press, 1973.

Sartre, Jean-Paul. *Literary and Philosophical Essays,* trans. Annette Michelson. London: Rider and Co., 1955.

Sidney, George. *Faulkner in Hollywood: A Study of His Career as a Scenarist.* Unpublished Ph.D. dissertation; University of New Mexico, 1959. (Available through University Microfilms.)

Slatoff, Walter. *Quest for Failure: A Study of William Faulkner.* Ithaca: Cornell University Press, 1960.

Spencer, Sharon. *Space, Time, and Structure in the Modern Novel.* New York: New York University Press, 1971.

Vickery, Olga. *The Novels of William Faulkner: A Critical Interpretation.* Baton Rouge: Louisiana State University Press, 1959.

Wilde, Meta Carpenter, and Orin Borstin. *A Loving Gentleman.* New York: Simon and Schuster, 1976.

Wood, Robin. *Howard Hawks.* Garden City: Doubleday and Co., 1968.

INDEX